ADVANCE PRAISE FOR *BEYOND SMARTER*

"Reuven Feuerstein is one of a handful of educational thinkers and practitioners who has made a significant, lasting contribution to our understanding of human learning."

—Howard Gardner,
Harvard Graduate School of Education

"America has the opportunity and obligation to fully develop the intellectual capital of all its students. Reuven Feuerstein has provided us with the antidote for the pernicious gap between intellectual potential and academic achievement that millions of our students experience."

—Yvette Jackson,
CEO, National Urban Alliance

"This book is a must-read for any individual who believes that there are no barriers to what a mind can learn to do, especially when aided by skilled mediators who believe deeply that brains can grow, minds can change, and intelligence is not fixed."

—James A. Bellanca,
CEO, International Renewal Institute, Inc.

"This book will make a valuable contribution to the intense debate concerning schooling in America and will help to effect change both systematically and individually. Whether you are a policymaker, a superintendent, a principal, or a classroom teacher, this book will give you both hope and practical knowledge. Feuerstein's work invites educators to focus on the radical improvement of mental capacities in the lives of students, regardless of the severity of the students' other difficulties. This book is a significant contribution to the national effort to improve schooling in America and to prepare our students for life in the 21st Century."

—Monsignor James E. Gilg,
Superintendent of Schools, Archdiocese of Omaha

GW00535812

BEYOND
SMARTER

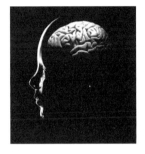

MEDIATED LEARNING AND THE
BRAIN'S CAPACITY FOR CHANGE

REUVEN FEUERSTEIN
REFAEL S. FEUERSTEIN
LOUIS H. FALIK

Foreword by John D. Bransford

TEACHERS
COLLEGE
PRESS

Teachers College
Columbia University
New York and London

The authors would like to thank David Herman,who performed the English translation of the material in this book, which was drawn from a series of radio broadcasts delivered in Hebrew by the lead author and subsequently published in Israel.

Published by Teachers College Press, 1234 Amsterdam Avenue, New York, NY 10027

Library of Congress Cataloging-in-Publication Data

Feuerstein, Reuven.
    Beyond smarter : mediated learning and the brain's capacity for change / Reuven Feuerstein, Refael S. Feuerstein, Louis H. Falik.
        p. cm.
    Includes bibliographical references and index.
    ISBN 978-0-8077-5118-3 (pbk. : alk. paper)
    ISBN 978-0-8077-5119-0 (hardcover : alk. paper)
    1. Educational psychology. 2. Learning—Physiological aspects. 3. Brain.
    4. Teaching—United States—Psychological aspects. I. Feuerstein, Refael S.
    II. Falik, Louis H. III. Title.
LB1051.F43 2010
370.15′2—dc22   2010011944

ISBN 978-0-8077-5118-3 (paper)
ISBN 978-0-8077-5119-0 (hardcover)

Printed on acid-free paper
Manufactured in the United States of America

17   16   15   14   13   12   11   10   8   7   6   5   4   3   2   1

THE AUTHORS DEDICATE THIS BOOK TO

the loving memory of Berta Guggenheim Feuerstein (Z''L);

our beloved wives Tal Ben-Ari Feuerstein and Marilynn Lubin Falik,
for their love, support, and ongoing dedication and engagement
in the meaning and manifestation of this work;

and to Malka Hoffman,
who dedicated her life to the promotion of
the applications of the work presented in this book.

Contents

Foreword

Reading this beautifully written book on theory and practice brought up a flood of warm and vivid memories from the mid-1970s, when I first met Professor Reuven Feuerstein and several members of his team. I was in the College of Arts and Sciences at Vanderbilt University and had heard that he was giving a talk at the John F. Kennedy Center, a major research institution at George Peabody College, Vanderbilt's esteemed school of education. Along with several students and colleagues, I decided to attend.

The talk was riveting. The preface to this book captures two of the major reasons why I was so moved by the talk. (The preface is in Professor Feuerstein's own words and they are much more eloquent than mine, so be sure to read it.) To foreshadow the discussion, you'll see that he emphasizes two major influences on his life's work: (1) Opportunities to work closely with major scholars—especially Jean Piaget and Andre Rey—and (2) the end of World War II and the subsequent challenge of helping child Holocaust survivors from across the world who were immigrating to Palestine, soon to become Israel.

Many of these youth seemed far less sophisticated developmentally than the youth who participated in studies that Professor Feuerstein had observed and conducted while working with Piaget and Rey, and this was often correlated with low scores. For example, on tests such as the Ravens Progressive Matrices (described later in this book). A natural and humanistic response to these low levels of performance—and many of Feuerstein's colleagues argued for this response with the best of intentions—was to carve out a set of societal niches where these people could be comfortable and become able to support themselves. But what kinds of societal niches? Many argued that they should require only menial skills. Feuerstein disagreed.

The question Feuerstein asked was: Does the possibility exist for a kind of cognitive modifiability that goes beyond helping people simply learn a particular set of facts and manual procedures and, instead, develops strategic context-sensitive skills, knowledge, identities, and habits of mind that transform their abilities to interact with others; to identify problems and turn them into opportunities for new learning; and to shape their environments when needed in order to make learning more effective? Could sensitive approaches to assessment, intervention (mediation), and opportunities for continued engagement in socially supportive environments allow people to continue to accelerate and expand their learning abilities over a lifetime? Feuerstein's answer to these questions was "yes," and his commitment to this answer prompted his theory of structural cognitive modifiability and the development of a suite of assessments and interventions for helping people succeed.

If you read the preface, you'll see that the idea of cognitive modifiability has been, and still is, often met with great resistance. Part of the reason, I think, is that it has been interpreted differently by various groups of people. Does it mean that one's goal should be to produce large changes in intelligence test scores for individuals? Does it mean that people can be helped to overcome self-doubts and impulsive, non-strategic habits of mind in order to free them to persist and experience more successful future learning? From what I saw, a focus on changes in intelligence test scores was not Feuerstein's major metric for success. One reason for this is that critics could say that he simply "taught to the test."

The second idea of cognitive modifiability that I discussed earlier is one that resonates with me personally and I think also with Professor Feuerstein. It fits numerous cases I have seen of Professor Feuerstein interacting with students and helping them change their confidence and strategies while also getting feedback from parents about encouraging changes in their children that fit more closely with this second perspective. Since modern researchers continue to find evidence that behavior affects brain development and not only vice versa, this second interpretation of cognitive modifiability is not simply a statement that, with practice, people can learn more knowledge and skills yet still remain at a fixed level of development. It is a much more powerful statement that supports the need for continued research on social support for modifiability and what it means and how it works.

It is noteworthy that the authors argue against the suggestion that they are proposing an "inoculation model," which assumes that once thinking is "fixed" through assessment-sensitive interventions, people will automatically be able to function at more complex levels for the rest of their lives. Instead, the authors emphasize the importance of shaping "post-intervention environments" that include tools, people, and other social and material resources for supporting, rather than blocking, continual positive change. This is a view that sees learning and development as dynamic and transactional, with multiple feedback loops that ideally sustain and accelerate ongoing learning as people go about their lives. Research on the nature of these kinds of environments is extremely timely and I'm eager to personally explore in more detail the deep and wise insights on this issue that Feuerstein and his colleagues share with us in this publication. Needless to say, the promising connections to new work in neuroscience represent additional leads that this book will help practitioners and researchers pursue. I hope to be one of them.

I am extremely happy to see this book published. It chronicles a brilliant and much-to-be-revered lifelong commitment to exploring issues of cognitive modifiability. I'm convinced that this foundational work will generate new practices among teachers and school leaders as well as productive discussions and new research trajectories as the field of learning progresses. I wish readers had the multiple opportunities that I have had to see Professor Feuerstein in action. He is a brilliant cognitive clinician, much in the spirit of his mentor, Andre Rey. I also wish people could interact with parents of students who have seen the benefits from the tireless work needed to help their children develop a sense of agency and competence that changes their life chances. These are the data—clinical data—that support a belief in this process.

Of course, clinical examples of success are wonderful to see, but many people feel they have their limitations—especially when one cannot meet the study participants in the flesh. As one of many researchers who has been keenly interested in helping Professor Feuerstein conduct rigorous studies of his theories and practices, I see in hindsight that the field as a whole—or at least a large subset of the field, including many researchers like myself—lacked the kinds of methodological tools and ways of thinking about data that are necessary to truly help Feuerstein and colleagues test and refine their fundamental ideas. In the mid-1970s, the spirit of the times involved a push for data in the form of increased scores on intelligence tests (hard to do in a short amount of time), strong "transfer" from Instrumental Enrichment to increasing success in academic learning, and so forth. Professor Feuerstein knew that these kinds of measures were too blunt to expect strong effects, but what were the alternatives?

The zeitgeist of today's learning sciences is much more conducive to conducting the kinds of research needed to more fully document and explore the processes involved in cognitive modifiability. New paradigms for research are opening up, including neuroscience, of course, but also ethnographic studies that carefully document how the same people often learn differently in a variety of informal and formal environments depending on a variety of learning stances and arrangements, how learning depends on both teacher and student beliefs as well as opportunities for just-in-time mentoring and collaboration, and so forth.

In my opinion these shifts in research paradigms make the theoretical work of Professor Feuerstein and his colleagues more important than ever. This is not unusual in science. For example, new theories of plate tectonics provided a mechanism for the movement of the Earth's crust that made older theories of continental drift much more important, plausible, and subject to exciting research. In the case of the theories of Feuerstein and colleagues, examples that make the theory more important than ever include new methods and approaches for studying the social and cultural nature of learning and adaptation (including its bases in brain) occurring in settings that are "lifelong, lifewide and lifedeep" (e.g., see Banks et. al, downloadable at LIFE-slc.org).

I close with a sincere thank you to Professor Feuerstein and colleagues for their highly innovative and immensely hope-inspiring work. By making his work accessible to practicing educators as well as to researchers, this new book can help teachers and leaders see their most challenging students in new ways, provide them with new understandings of how thinking occurs, help them to see and identify specific stage and task specific kinds of thinking in their students, and support growth in all students toward more skillful thinking. Overall, this book provides both researchers and practitioners with a treasure map for additional exciting and vibrant teaching, along with metrics for judging successful learning, and research.

—John D. Bransford,
Shauna C. Larson Professor of the Learning Sciences,
University of Washington; and co-director of the
Center for Learning in Informal and Formal Environments (LIFE)

Preface

In this book we shall deal with the human being's capacity for cognitive modifiability and how this ability of the brain/mind to change informs the way we can help students improve their ability to think and learn. We raise and answer the critical questions relating to students'—or any human being's—ability to change, and be changed by, experience. It is an interesting and important issue that continues to be controversial in the fields of education, psychology, and social policy. After many years in which the question was not addressed—more recently in response and reaction to the development of cognitive psychology and changes in the sociopolitical climate—a number of books have appeared that have voiced sharp opposition to the possibility of changing intelligence—or in our words, the individual's thinking ability. However, in a positive vein, these positions have also aroused a storm of counter-reactions, arguments, and discussions, which in themselves testify to the importance that is today attached to the issues—to the nature, development, and capacity for intelligence and learning, and the role of thinking skills as factors that determine a person's fate in the development of human society.

From a historical standpoint, two totally different encounters led me (Reuven Feuerstein) to develop the theory of structural cognitive modifiability (SCM): first, my exposure to Jean Piaget, who can be described as the modern founder of developmental cognitive psychology; and second, my encounters and responses with the children who survived the Holocaust during World War II in Europe.

While a student and participant in the Geneva Institute of Jean Piaget, I encountered Professor Andre Rey, a member of the faculty of the Institute. Because of Professor Rey's creative mind, and his early conceptualizations of alternative approaches to the assessment of learning and cognitive functions, I received encouragement and support to develop my work. This encouraged me to think about the processes and potential to change intellective and cognitive functions and to assess them in new and different ways. Andre Rey was my mentor and became my colleague. He came with me to meet the children of the Holocaust and worked with me there and in Israel to further develop techniques and interventions.

In my work with Piaget, who was one of the great believers in the decisive influence of thinking on the human being's adaptive processes, I brought a perspective influenced by my knowledge of the then-influential dynamic psychology of Freud, Jung, and the somewhat lesser-known Szondi. These were the major points of view at the time, in the early 1950s, and they attributed the main causes of human behavior to uncontrollable inclinations and drives originating in the subconscious mind. For example, Szondi believed heredity played a decisive influence on a person's behavior and all of his or her choices. He coined the term *operotropism,* referring to the unconscious inclinations that we possess for certain areas of involvement.

This history is recounted here because it points to the extent to which the early psychodynamic psychologists attached very little importance to the cognitive system, which contains the thinking functions and oversees information-processing, and foregrounds my early need to challenge these assumptions. I began to argue against the point of view that the impulses that guided behavior (and learning) were largely emotional in origin and that the thinking component—the ability to organize one's perception, to collect data, and to turn it into new sources of knowledge—was negligible.

Presenting a theoretical alternative to the emotional conceptualization were the behaviorists, who focused almost exclusively on behavior and its outcomes and showed no interest in its origins. In the final analysis, they too left very little room for thinking itself.

What were the consequences of this dichotomy? People with a high mental capacity constituted ostensible proof of the marginality of thinking ability on the development of personality and mental structures—they had the skills and propensities as a consequence of their dynamic histories, and there was nothing much you could do for them. Many even argued that it was disturbing to attempt to intervene in such situations. Educators who were influenced by these psychodynamic energetic concepts with regard to the functioning of the human being felt that it was their responsibility simply to liberate the powers of children and to refine their impulses. They did not consider thinking to be an important factor for connecting the stimuli experienced, nor did they consider how what the person derives from experience can become a factor regulating responsive behavior.

In Piaget, I found an island of thought about the cognitive system. Piaget asked, for example, how children construct their worlds by means of thinking and acting as determined by the maturation of the brain and acting according to the relevance of the objects to which the individual is exposed. According to Piaget, the cognitive system develops structures and operations of thinking that are created in the course of interactions between the self and the world at various stages of development and maturation. These thinking structures (Piaget called them schemata) enable a person to organize the world that is experienced and plan it, to create new information from what is not experienced directly, and to build in thought an expanded world that is planned and organized.

Piaget's theory planted in me the hope and potential for helping child Holocaust survivors. My encounter with them constituted a second source of the theory of structural cognitive modifiability. I first met the child Holocaust survivors in 1944 and 1945, when I myself was a new immigrant to what was then Palestine and was later to become the state of Israel. I arrived in Mikve Yisrael as an instructor. It was the first residential agricultural school that received children from the Holocaust, and its major goal was to rehabilitate them from their traumatic experiences. I found myself among children who had undergone a very traumatic period in an illogical, disorderly, and brutal world without the means of adaptation. I had worked with such children in Bucharest before becoming an immigrant myself. In both cases, I asked myself how it would be possible to create thinking processes in such children, and I wondered about the significance of thinking as a means of processing the chaotic world they had lived in. I was with them during the nights when they relived all the horrors they had gone through, and I asked myself, "How will I be able to speak to them, tomorrow morning, about what they had learned, or about Bible chapters, or about any other study subject?" The question that bothered me most of all was: Were these children capable of change, after all that they had been through?

In Piaget's theory, through the importance that he attached to the thinking element, I found confirmation of the possibility of drawing these children out of the chaos and of building for them a new life through the rehabilitation of their thought mechanisms.

Piaget's great contribution was in adding to the magma—to the central nucleus of life, made up of emotions, inclinations, and drives—the emergent cognitive skills that could be assumed to be gradually created from it. Following my understanding of Piaget, and my previous experiences, I came to recognize the need to give thinking—the mind and an active and interactive intelligence that organizes the world and plans ahead—a central position in a person's life.

This book, and the rationale, theories, and practices developed herein, is the outcome of this need and the struggles that ensued. In the opening chapters of this book we raise three questions, which have guided the development of my work and that will accompany us throughout this book.

The first question is: *What is the significance of thinking as a decisive factor in determining the human beings' behavior, its place, its status, and its contribution to achievements in society?*

The second question is: *Is it possible to modify thinking?* That is to say, can one change the intelligence and ways of learning of a person, or are they like the weather, which we often talk about but about which nothing can be done?

Assuming that intelligence plays an important role in determining the level of a person's functioning, and assuming that, in fact, one can change one's functioning, the question must be asked, and this is our third question: *How do we do it? How do we modify a person's functioning?*

These three questions have proven to be relevant not only for children of the Holocaust, who were my first concern, but also for culturally deprived and culturally different children, and children with chromosomal and genetic deficits. Modifiability applies to them and can be applied to a wide and diverse range of human conditions. This book is about the answers to these questions. Our goal is to present this in such a way as to be accessible to parents, teachers, and all others who have a need and an interest in the concepts and potential of modifiability to improve the human condition.

The terms *mediator* and *teacher* are not used interchangeably in this book. Teachers must often transmit knowledge and skills, as must parents. Mediation is an intentional interaction with the learner, the purpose of which is to enhance the learner's understanding beyond the immediate experience and to help the learner to apply what is learned in broader contexts—goals that often go beyond the simple transmission of knowledge, but which are necessary enhancements. However, it is important to understand—as is discussed in several chapters of this book—that parents are the first and intuitive mediators of the world for their children, and teachers have the opportunity to play the same role with their students. This book is designed to enable both teachers and parents to become more intentional and knowledgeable in this process and to capitalize on the power and meaningfulness of mediated learning experience. We hope that readers will come to understand the term *mediator* to include a wide range of potential. For readers who wish to study this material further, we have compiled an annotated bibliography at the end of the book.

This book originated in a series of lectures that the senior author gave on Israeli radio almost a decade ago. Whenever the text refers to "I," it is the voice and experience of the senior author, Reuven Feuerstein. The original lectures have been expanded for this book, bringing forth the considerable further developments in theory, concept, practice, and neuroscientific research that have occurred in the almost decade since the original lectures were conceived and delivered.

Acknowledgments

We first express our thanks to the publishers of the original volume of lectures upon which this book is based. Their willingness and desire to bring this material to a wider population indicates a commitment to human values and educational and social change. We are especially grateful to Tirtza Youval (Z''L), who served as editor for publications of the "University of the Radio," an early provider of what is now well known as "distance learning." Ariella Sturm served as editor for the Hebrew language book.

The authors are indebted to Mr. David Herman who translated the original Hebrew text into English. His good spirits, ready engagement, and attention to both detail and nuance have facilitated our work on this manuscript, allowing a depth of focus and clarity of content that would not have been otherwise possible.

Kathleen (Kate) Bellanca brought us into contact with the editors of Teachers College Press, particularly Jean Ward, and has acted as a communications liaison for the authors with Jean, who has become one of the main editors of this volume. Both Kate and Jean deserve our thanks for their belief in the project and their timely responses and prodding that brought this project to its fruition.

CHAPTER 1

The Role of Thinking in Learning

The first question that we address in this chapter is: Is thinking so important that we should be intensively concerned about it, and does it require significant changes in methods of education? Our answer is affirmative. As a society we are facing the needs of populations and new and demanding conditions of life that require the structuring of thinking and its development. Later in this book we will define and describe what we mean by thinking. But for now, let's take an overview. Many individuals from diverse cultures find themselves chained to restrictive ways of thinking, have limited options for adaptation, and possess meager resources to initiate life-sustaining changes.

We can even say this about those societies and situations that provide all of the modern advantages and conveniences, including—as a particularly salient example—the many children who come from affluent homes and seem to lack nothing. Yet these children demonstrate a low level of functioning. We will define intelligence at this early point in our discussion as the ability to think adaptively in response to changes in our environment. It has a decisive impact on human beings' ability to choose, to plan ahead, make decisions in a rational manner, and to organize the data they gather and possess in an order of priority. These abilities are required today more than ever because human beings find themselves confronted with decision crossroads that were not previously faced. In the past, many children and adults were confronted with externally determined decisions, a limited range of choices, and much simpler and straightforward variables from which to choose. Today, a person has to decide for him- or herself in the face of a multitude of choices. It has been said that the modern person is exposed to more stimuli in a 24-hour period than medieval man was exposed to in his entire lifetime. Therefore, one must be equipped with the tools required in order to decide upon and differentiate among numerous and almost overwhelming options. If one is not conscious of the need for these tools and the ability to use them, one is likely to reach decisions from emotional drives and impulses that do not always work to one's benefit, or to the benefit of the community in which one lives. The development of thinking and the development of the orientation toward it constitute a most important educational objective—today more than ever.

IS COGNITION IMPORTANT? AND IF SO, WHY?

In response to the first question we have raised, we have identified ten reasons why cognition represents a needed focus on learning for the present and future of human development (Feuerstein and Falik, 2000). These reasons apply to learning both in the educational context and throughout life.

1. Perception is irreversible; cognition is adaptive and changeable.
2. Cognition permits the individual to control the environment at ever greater distances from the immediately perceived and experienced. This means that with cognition, one does not have to directly experience an object or event, but can "think about it" and deal with it from a distance. This expands greatly one's options in dealing with the world.
3. Cognitive processes help us to decide what to focus on, when to focus, and in what ways to focus. This is very important if one is presented with too many or conflicting stimuli that attract our attention.
4. Cognitive processes help the individual to organize and sequence the great amount of information that comes into the system, enabling planning, decision making, and bringing order to potentially diverse and disconnected experiences.
5. Cognitive processes transform the data that is gathered into mental structures to be reframed or elaborated later. As we think about what we have experienced, we can adapt our experiences to new conditions and use them in ways beyond or different from the original exposure.
6. Cognitive processes generate new information not limited to what is derived from existent sources of information. This is yet another example of the necessary distance one needs from direct experiences.
7. Once conceptualization occurs (structures created through cognitive processes) it can be communicated to others. Sharing experiences and understandings becomes an important aspect of cultural transmission and adaptation.
8. Cognitive processes enable access to the affective—emotional-attitudinal dimensions of human experience—what is commonly referred to as motivation. This moves human experience into the important aspects of why we do what we do, and the deeper meaning of our experiences, and energizes positive movement in human growth and development.
9. Cognitive processes are in a constant state of animation, producing consciousness. Meaningful adaptation to the world requires that one has an awareness of the need and the motivation to change, often in the face of potential stress or conflict.
10. Cognitive processes enable recognition of conflicts, acceptance of dissonance, and generation of productive conflicts that expand consciousness and initiate activity to address them.

Thus, these cognitive processes that we have just described are necessary components for our students to respond to our age of rapid change. Units of behavior were once transmitted to us prepared in advance, and not only was it unnecessary to change them, it was even forbidden to change them too much. The use of these "behavioral units" did not derive from the will of the individual or from choice. The context of the times forced certain types of thinking and responding on the individual, created the conditions necessary to continue to use them, and often generated forces that restricted adaptive responding. Today, the individual cannot use modes of action prepared in advance. Even when they can be used initially, they must be employed with great discretion and adapted to the given situation, and care must be given to the decisions that are made on how specifically to respond. These decisions, which are everyday occurrences for us, cannot be the responsibility of others. They cannot be assumed to happen automatically and without the acquisition of strategies and skills—what we refer to as the tools of thinking.

WHAT ARE
THE TOOLS OF THINKING?

A student has to be equipped with thinking abilities that include correct perception, proper data collection, sensitivity to problems, properly identifying and defining situations to be responded to, solving those problems, and making rational, grounded decisions. Furthermore, the rapid tempo of change confronts a person today with a very intensive demand to adjust through learning. One has to acquire new forms of functioning in order to be able to meet new requirements created in the workplace and in the environment in the wake of technological and other developments. Ever-changing, newly framed options open before the individual, and choices cannot be made without the processes of self-adaptation and modification. We must prepare students for this reality.

We maintain that the cognitive component is a most important element in the development of a human being's personality. Therefore, a critical question must be asked: Is it possible to equip a person with thinking tools that are essential for a sound adaptation to life, even when they are lacking, to one degree or another? When we come to address this question, there are two possibilities before us.

The first one is to follow the existing tendencies and to accept the ability as an innate, unmodifiable element that is inherited in certain and predetermined quantities. This can be called a *fixist* point of view. To someone who adopts this view, it remains only to answer the question negatively, as do many psychologists and educators who believe that significant changes cannot be made. According to this point of view, human beings cannot be changed, at least beyond a certain peripheral level. People's behaviors—the way they function and their decisions—are determined by their genetic inheritance and neurological system, and only a small part of their responses are created by educational-environmental processes and individual decisions.

Of course, we choose the second possibility and answer the question that was asked in the affirmative. In the following chapters, we shall present a theory that views students as modifiable creatures and responds to them as such. This theory posits that students are not only modifiable, but that they modify themselves and their environments structurally. That is to say, the changes that we shall describe are not random or limited in time or space, but present opportunities for changing the basic structures (both behaviorally and neurophysiologically) that are responsible for a person's thinking and behavioral processes. Our optimism in this regard has been strengthened by the new neurophysiology—specifically the discovery of evidence for neuroplasticity, with mechanisms such as the mirror neurons. We will summarize this evidence and relate it to our theories and approaches in Chapter 14 of this book.

In this book, we shall be dealing mainly with the cognitive system, but it is important to point out clearly that emotion, from our standpoint, is the energetic basis, the driving force, and the answer to the questions, Why do I (or don't I) do what I do? As we have noted above, cognition directs us to modulate and control our emotions. There is practically no behavior that does not have both an emotional motivation and a cognitive element, but the cognitive factor fulfills a very important function in bringing in the higher-order emotions and profound moral and ethical differentiations.

We believe, therefore, that cognitive processes can be very powerful in changing the emotional/energetic determinants of behavior. Cognitive processes make the individual modifiable. We maintain that there exist mutually influential relations between intelligence and emotion. Piaget used the metaphor of "two sides of the same coin" to compare the relationship between them. Emotion is the energetic factor, the driving impulse that determines *why* to do something and that creates the need to do something. The cognitive elements of intelligence guide the person toward *what* to do. Said another way, these elements facilitate the structuring of behavior, responding to questions of *when*, *how*, and *where* do I act/respond/internalize my behavior. That is to say, my behavior is a product of these two components—the emotional element is the energetic factor and the intellective (cognitive) element is the factor that builds the structure of behavior.

Our basic assumption that human beings are modifiable creatures relates to most of their traits, including those that are often or usually considered to be pathological (dysfunctional, rigid, and so forth) and inherited to some degree. We maintain that these elements are also amenable to modifiability. This assumption, which is not accepted by all those who deal with human behavior, expresses a very optimistic message. However, at the same time, it also places a heavy responsibility on human beings and on their environment. We, as human beings, are capable of changing ourselves and our fate; but the responsibility for this rests on us, and on the environment we are in. This refers to all of the significant others in the life of the individual, including parents, teachers, caretakers, support professionals, and the institutional decision makers who create the conditions for modifiability.

Where we go with this and how we materialize our responsibilities is the subject of this book. We shall consider a theoretical perspective that supports our approach, and then we will describe the applications and outcomes that are produced when one assumes the propensity for modifiability and focuses on the development of thinking skills and strategies to stimulate cognition. In this sense this book is both theoretical and practical. In fact, it is our fundamental position that one needs both theory and practice. How we develop concepts guides our practices, and what we do (our practices) contributes to the shaping of our theory.

CHAPTER 2

The Human Being Is Modifiable!

In the first chapter we described the importance of the quality of intelligence that influences the way in which a person functions and of the emotional-energetic source of functioning. In this chapter we address our second question: Are these two components of intelligence, the intellect and the emotion, modifiable?

We begin our answer from what may seem an unusual perspective, that of an expression of *faith*. This word is used despite the fact that from a position of *science* one has the inclination and training to divest oneself completely from such an "unscientific" term. But the point we wish to emphasize is that in the beginning there must be a *need*—a need that will generate the belief in human modifiability. I must have the need to have my students and those with whom I am engaged reach higher potentials of functioning. This need energizes me to act and motivates my faith (belief) that there are positive, effective, and meaningful alternatives to be found, to fight for, and to bring this faith into being.

Here we introduce the concept of the belief system and its critical place in the development and actualization of the theory of structural cognitive modifiability. I must *believe* that the student is a modifiable being who is capable of change and capable of changing according to his or her will and decisions. Human beings' modifiability differentiates them from other creatures and, according to the *Rabbinic Midrash*, "even from the angels." Herein lies the main uniqueness of human beings.

By the term *change* we do not mean the acquisition of 20 words in some language or even the acquisition of a complex skill like piloting an airplane, although for a given individual these may be meaningful acquisitions. We mean changes in the structure of thinking—for example, creating for the individual *the necessary conditions* to acquire new words in order to create in the process of thinking new things that had not previously entered the mind. We assume that a person is capable of acquiring for him- or herself not only quantities of knowledge or skills but also new cognitive structures, by which are opened new areas that were not previously included in the stockpile of knowledge and abilities.

When we talk about human beings' modifiability, we assume that this ability enables the acquisition of additional abilities that were not previously present or accessible. We are not referring to abilities that are the result of developmental age, mental maturation, or of the response to developmental experiences. These relatively direct learning experiences enable students to use their accumulated experience in order to repeat successful actions and to avoid mistakes. We differentiate those types of changes, which give a different character to their experiences and enable the understanding of their experiences, from changes that lead one to interact with the world differently than what had been previously experienced. This type of substantive change requires a whole array of thinking strategies and perspectives about the manner of its taking place—how to attend to stimuli, how to operate (manipulate, sequence, compare, and so forth). We shall discuss this conceptualization in greater detail in due course.

Our optimistic view of the human potential for modifiability arouses much amazement, which people direct not only at us (for developing this point of view) but also at themselves. We have observed a curious ambiguity of feeling with regard to the potential for modifiability. To accept oneself capable of change involves taking risks—one might not be successful, one might make mistakes, one is not familiar with the newly modified self. Thus, one enters the unfamiliar. There is the very real fear of being alienated from oneself—an existential danger. Mediated learning experience (MLE) is aware of and addresses itself specifically and systematically to this resistance, and MLE works actively to overcome it. We address ourselves to these issues throughout this book (particularly in Chapters 6 and 7) and with special reference to the effects of these variables from our knowledge from the new neurosciences in Chapter 14.

This unique ability of a student or adult to modify him- or herself exists as an option. We emphasize the word *option* because it reminds us that not everyone actualizes this ability. It exists as a possibility; in order to actualize it, an investment of effort and resources is required. But the option exists for all individuals, whoever they may be, even when barriers or obstacles stand in the way of its implementation.

BARRIERS ON THE WAY TO REALIZING MODIFIABILITY

Three barriers are liable to stand in the way of students' realization of their modifiability: the etiological barrier (the cause of conditions of deficit or dysfunction), the barrier of age of onset (the age at which the barrier was identified and the intervention initiated), and the barrier produced by the severity of the person's condition. But these barriers can be overcome, as we shall describe below. To recognize the importance of overcoming these barriers through the process of modifiability, it is necessary to understand each of them, and specifically their impact on the provision of activities supporting modifiability.

The Etiological Barrier

The term *etiology* refers to a great diversity of causes. Some of these causes are organic and originate in the biological structure of human beings, and they are considered responsible for dysfunctional conditions (including many that are cognitive in nature). Some of these causes are developmental, occurring over time and in the course of biological/maturational processes, and others may be acquired conditions. For example, damage caused as a result of a stroke or conditions occurring due to lack of oxygen during birth are acquired conditions; while the diverse chromosomal disorders creating syndromes or genetic aberrations such as Down syndrome or Fragile X are developmental. Historically and presently, these manifestations of various etiological conditions are considered as ruling out the option of human beings' modifiability. It was assumed that these were insurmountable barriers because it was considered, for example, impossible to change a person's chromosomes or to make good the lack of oxygen that occurred during the process of birth. In the past, it was assumed that brain damage was also irreparable because the brain was not considered capable of renewing its nervous system. Today, we now have strong and growing evidence from the "new brain sciences" that this is a mistaken assumption, as we describe in the final chapter of this book. But, essentially, the evidence for *neuroplasticity* provides a strong support for the potential to overcome these etiological barriers.

According to our theory of structural cognitive modifiability (SCM), we assume that although etiological barriers may exist, they can be overcome through the application of mediated learning experience (MLE).

A journalist from the French publication *Le Monde* knew of our work with Down syndrome children whom we brought to higher levels of functioning. In response to MLE and exposure to cognitive modifiability interventions, many of these young people were able to complete their educations and become artists, poets, and so forth. This journalist wrote that, for us, "the chromosomes don't have the last word." It is our belief and experience that a human being who possesses the need, belief, intention, and the proper tools can be given a way to bypass the barriers of etiology and realize the option of modifiability.

Etiological barriers may also be environmental, emotional, a result of cultural deprivation and cultural differences that may result in early childhood deprivation, educational failures, and the like. Many think that even these external (exogenous) factors determine a lack of the potential for modifiability. We of course know otherwise!

The Age Barrier

Frequent mention is made of a *critical age*, which sets a barrier for a person. In psychology, the concept of *critical period* is well-known and accepted. This view holds that if a person has not achieved certain functions—for example, the development of language, reading, or higher-order thinking functions—by a certain generally established age the necessary learning ability for adaptation and the behaviors that will enable functioning have little chance of being modified.

The assumption that supports the position of a critical period is derived from an *organismic* conception, according to which intelligence is the product of organic structures in the brain—a matter of our physiology. From this perspective, it is assumed that the brain reaches the height of its maturation at a certain age, and that after a period of stability, the next phase is a process of declining ability. Therefore, the option given to a human being to develop is temporally limited, and if certain growth has not occurred—"if the time has passed"—there will no longer be any possibilities to change, irrespective of how much intervention is offered to the individual. From this point of view, there is a natural acceptance of decline in abilities, or limited potential to affect changes in functions after the passage of the critical period. Here, too, the existence of neuroplasticity heavily supports the potential to affect changes in functions, overcoming the limitations presumably due to having passed the critical period for development.

In the past, this perspective was (and in many quarters still is) widely accepted and led to a concentration of efforts for the development of human beings at a tender age. Programs intended for adolescent and young adults were either reduced or abolished so as to have resources available for those young children who were presumed most able to benefit. (It was considered "too late" for some and a waste of money for the others.)

Such investment in young children is welcome and needed! However, there was a misperception of the necessity and effects of this investment, as it was seen as creating a kind of immunization. That is to say, some thought that if we invest in children of tender age, we shall ostensibly immunize them against the difficulties of life they will subsequently encounter, and we can relax (e.g., cease providing) our intervention efforts at later stages. However, the long-term results did not always live up to expectations; the early investment that was terminated (prematurely, in our opinion) did not produce the hoped-for immunization, especially when the interventions for older children were neglected. In the United States, this led to the reductions of Head Start programs for young children because the long-term outcome effects were considered to be disappointing—the Head Start children did not presumably (according to some standards) maintain their gains following their termination of the program—of course, with no further follow-up support with their learning or development.

An Example of Challenging the "Critical Period" Concept

The critical period for learning to speak is considered to be approximately 7 years of age. However, we have had direct experiences that challenge this conclusion: Alex, a young man we have described extensively elsewhere in our writings, did not learn to speak until the age of 9, following an extensive surgical procedure that excised the entire left hemisphere of his brain. Incidentally, after learning to speak he went on to acquire a wide range of language-based cognitive and academic functions—much against his neurologists' expectations and predictions, and following several years of conventional attempts to teach him to read and write that were unsuccessful.

We believe (again, we use—not by chance—the term "belief") that human beings are modifiable during the entire course of their lifetimes and can create wonderful changes even at advanced ages. This ability was examined and served as a basis for different research studies that rejected the notion that a person's modifiability is blocked at a certain age; the time of cognitive development is not identical with the time of the development of the skeleton and bones. Recent research studies conducted with a modified version of the Feuerstein Instrumental Enrichment (FIE) program, which we built to improve a person's learning ability (namely, to produce cognitive change), have proved that people can indeed change even when they are very old. Alex continued to change and develop, acquiring not only language but also higher-order cognitive functions well after his surgery and in response to very intensive and systematic interventions. Here again we find strong support for this modifiability from the revolutionary insights we have gained from the new neurosciences.

We can continue to develop in ourselves qualities and forms of thinking and skills that we didn't possess at earlier stages of our lives, even at a very advanced age. An important by-product of this change is in the emotional/energetic domain. People experiencing these changes feel more optimistic, powerful, engaged, and ready to further advance their cognitive functions.

Severity of Condition as a Barrier

There are severe multiple handicaps—physical, sensory, and mental—that place in question a person's modifiability. We must admit that, because we are optimistic by nature and in our theoretical perspectives, we also believed that there existed some cases where a real chance for meaningful change might not be possible. However, our experience working with populations with these handicaps proved that even the barrier of severity is not insurmountable. Of course, as indicated earlier, one must have a need and a belief that the barrier can be surmounted.

The case of Y. is a fine illustration of a human being's modifiability despite the severity of his or her condition:

> Y. came to me with a very severe disorder. She had a "birdlike"
> face, with bulging eyes, a long nose, and a tendency to twist her

head to the side so as to visually focus. She was not only unable to speak, but also lacked the ability to produce sounds other than a high-pitched wail that did not appear to be related to any overt experience to stimuli to which she was exposed. And it was impossible to teach her to put out her tongue. She suffered from *apraxia*—a disorder marked by the inability to perform certain physical movements like copying. She also suffered from *aboulia*—the inability to bring herself to initiate actions. That is, she had to receive strength from an external source in order to perform any kind of action. For instance, in order to get her to lift a cup, someone had to take her hand and get her to act. Without this, she would cease the action in the middle.

When I began to examine her, it seemed to me that nothing could be done. I gave up. I did not believe that anything could be changed. But the mother, who was very unhappy, did not give up. She had a great need: "I came to you because I thought that you could help. You have helped so many others. I cannot accept that my child will be an idiot! If you cannot do it, please teach me and I will do it!"

And so she came to me year after year, several times each year, in order to receive instruction from me on how to work with her daughter. After three and a half years she brought her to me again and said: "The girl is reading!" I treated the mother's words with great skepticism and said to myself "another dream of a mother who dearly wishes, a kind of wishful thinking." But the mother brought out a magnetic board with letters and the girl arranged them with one hand into words, sentences, and so on. Although I had taught the mother how to work with Y., I could not believe my eyes! I have to admit that this was for me a rather hard slap in the face, since I asked myself what would have happened had I believed that it was possible to change the girl's condition, and had I worked with her directly. We then began to work directly with her. We sat Y. down next to a computer and she reached amazing heights of writing with it.

She wrote a wonderful autobiography, and it turned out that she had grasped and understood everything that had been said around her, all the despair that had been expressed about her. When I asked her why her mother held her hand while she was typing on the computer, she wrote me in reply: "Honorable and respected Sir Professor . . . "—and I felt the irony in her words— "had you also been like me, if they had told you that you were an imbecile, that you were incapable of anything, and that only your mother believed in you and brought to you to do things as my mother has done, you too, Sir Professor, would not give her up."

THE IMPORTANCE OF
GENERATING THE BELIEF SYSTEM BASED ON NEEDS

Y.'s case brings us back to the matter of having a need and commitment leading to belief. This case clarifies why we use the term `belief`. Even when I have sufficient empirical and theoretical evidence regarding a human being's modifiability—for example, the mother's belief, which came from emotional involvement, from a sense of responsibility toward her daughter, and from her need and a fierce desire to see her gain a human quality of life—this belief is what creates the strength to look for the means to achieve results such as what the mother achieved. This means that we cannot be content with theoretical assumptions about modifiability, because a need is also required—an involvement and commitment toward helping the student achieve a higher quality of life. Only then will it be possible to surmount the barriers and for the option for change to be realized and become a reality.

CHAPTER 3

Changing the Structure of Learning and Behavior

In previous chapters, we dealt with cognition, which we define as the central factor in shaping human behavior, and we referred to the *structural* nature of the changes that can occur in this element. In this chapter we describe what is meant by the structural nature of change and identify the characteristics that make it structural. *Change that is structural will affect learning and behavior in deep, sustaining, and self-perpetuating ways.*

The first quality is described in the following way: *Every change that takes place in a part changes the whole to which it belongs.* That is to say, if I ask a child not only to answer the question I put to him, but also to give me two sensible reasons for the answer, I draw attention to the task. The task is changed so that the child must go beyond the simple answer (solution to the problem) and will search for an explanation for the answer, thereby finding a deeper meaning. And if a structural change is created, it will not remain confined to that event alone but will be given expression in many additional events that have similar or projected elements.

THE NATURE OF STRUCTURAL CHANGE

Piaget described cognitive processes whereby new cognitive schema (inner organizations of information and meaning) are assimilated and remain stable even when they are applied to new situations. But, they have the capability of expanding in order to adapt themselves to additional situations in a dual process of assimilation (taking in) and accommodation (adaptation to new or different situations).

That is, if one learns some principle, and a structural change occurs, one will be able to apply it in numerous and various instances where the same principle applies. Although the new instances will be different from one another in their form, size, importance, and so on, they will be responded to with regard to the similarity of their guiding principle.

Structural change is characterized by its tendency to continue to operate even after the initial factor that caused it is no longer directly experienced—

a quality that we have termed *cognitive distance*. When human beings change structurally, a disposition is created that enables them to go on changing in ways that are very hard to predict. One of the central assumptions of the theory of structural cognitive modifiability (SCM) is expressed in this quality of creating structural change, according to which a human being is both adaptive and unpredictable. When the change that occurs is liable to continue beyond what it was in the beginning, the capacity to change structurally turns the human being into an entity about whom neither the manner in which it will continue to exist nor the direction of its development can be predicted. This is the quality of adaptability and self-perpetuation.

DIMENSIONS OF STRUCTURAL CHANGE

The structural changes that are produced are not identical in magnitude or quality from one learner to another or from one situation to another. They must be observed, assessed, and innovatively manipulated. They can be described according to four parameters:

- *Permanence:* to what extent is the change preserved over time.
- *Resistance:* how resistant is the change to changed conditions and environments.
- *Flexibility/Adaptability:* to what extent is it included, beyond the initial situation, in other areas of learning responses and events.
- *Generalizability/Transformability:* to what extent does the individual continue to be modified and create new structural changes through independent efforts.

These dimensions of structural change are extremely important. We have derived the aims of our work and the specific tools of intervention to achieve them. We shall describe each one of them in more detail below.

Permanence, or Preservation of the Change

This dimension of structural change describes the ability of the learner to retain or preserve what has been learned. That is to say, if a structural change has occurred, the learner will be able to solve the problem, using the acquired strategies and operations the next day and long after that. On the other hand, if the change is not structural, each problem is encountered as though it were a fresh and new experience. The learner returns to previous thinking schemata, repeats errors, and needs to be taught (mediated) again. An excellent example of this quality of change is in those individuals who have been mediated on the Complex Figure Drawing (from the Learning Propensity Assessment Device—LPAD) and then asked to recall it after considerable time delays. If the learning has been structurally integrated, the design is recalled with high degrees of accuracy many months following the learning, even in situations where the learner had to overcome significant motor or cognitive deficits and required intensive mediation—perhaps because of the MLE applied!

Resistance to the Change

This variant relates to the questions: Will the learner preserve what has been learned even if we change the data of the problem and increase its complexity? Is the principle acquired shockproof, and is that which is learned able to resist the changed elements of the new situation, enabling the utilization of that which has been learned in spite of the differences encountered? These new elements have the potential to distract or confuse the learner if sufficient cognitive structure is not in place. The structural learning is the constant element. For example, let us assume that the learner has acquired the principle according to which 3 + 2 = 5, but it is lost when the order of the data is changed (2 + 3 = ?), or the modality of the problem is changed from numerical to verbal (three apples and two oranges equal how many pieces of fruit?). In such instances, what has been learned is resistant to the change in the conditions.

Flexibility of the Change

This variant is the opposite of resistance, in that the learner applies the acquired behavior in conditions that differ from those where retention was observed. This is the quality of *adaptability*. Here we refer to the plasticity of change when the learner must respond to tasks and conditions that no longer permit or require the application of the learned behavior with the same frequency, purpose, or goal. If the same behavior that was successful in a previous problem-solving situation is applied again and is not adapted to the new or changed situation, the inflexibility manifested suggests that the cognitive changes are insufficiently structured. In this way, cognitive structures are not simply internalized templates of response to be utilized in the same way every time but have a quality of adaptive application built into them.

As an example of this dimension, consider the child who has successfully learned addition and is able to flexibly activate the structural change that has taken place. There will be a readiness to grasp more easily the fundamental principle of the act of subtraction, and perhaps the child may even develop it on his or her own and apply it to the operations of multiplication and division. If the change has been integrated into the cognitive structure in both the structural areas of flexibility and generalization (see below), the development will not stop at the point where we left the learner, but will perpetuate on its own.

Generalization of the Change

This quality of change represents the highest level of structural change and relates to the questions: Will the learner manage to create structural changes on his or her own, and has there been created in the learner an orientation toward abstract thinking—that is, can the learner extract from the solution of a concrete problem the principle or rule that can be applied to new problems in other fields of application? Can the learner do this insightfully and spontaneously?

For example, let us assume that I have learned 10 words in English. If the change was not only quantitative (that is, 10 words have been added to my vocabulary), but I have also learned how to understand the words in the context of a whole sentence, a structural change has taken place in me that will change my whole approach to language and will determine the way I will continue to learn it. Moreover, it will direct me to seek out and pay attention to stimuli in the world to which I was exposed, and I will bring new and innovative cognitive insights to them, thereby deepening my understanding and expanding my perspective. We sometimes refer to this quality as a *transformation*, whereby stimuli and experiences are changed in some ways related to the generalizations we have formulated.

Generalization has a potentially unwelcome aspect—overgeneralization. For instance, if my grandfather has a beard, every man that I see who has a beard may be perceived by me as my grandfather. I might make the incorrect association that "all grandfathers have beards" or that "someone without a beard cannot be a grandfather." Thus, we want to control the generalization, to develop flexible and accurate relationships so that the learner is able to identify relevant characteristics and differentiate those that are distinguishing for the particular instance of the comparison.

DIFFERENTIATING THE NATURE OF CHANGE

Changes that take place are not always positive. Changes may also occur for the worse, and it is not always possible to predict them—or their direction—in advance. Students sometimes decline in their level of functioning and lose abilities that they have attained. Because human beings are responsible for their destinies, students must always be on their guard—yesterday's good functioning does not guarantee that the same will be the case tomorrow. But this coin has two sides: Students can also be encouraged that the low functioning of yesterday does not preclude the chances of attaining higher achievement tomorrow. It is this expectation of positive change, and the willingness (of the mediator) to push for change, that maintains a positive and optimistic engagement that stimulates and encourages change, even when regressions or lack of change have been experienced.

It appears, therefore, as though a human being's cognitive system is not only modifiable but also subject to structural change—that is, a change that is deep, enduring, and also dynamic and amenable to development beyond that which has been previously experienced and learned.

This conception stands in considerable contradiction to that currently held by many in the behavioral sciences, whereby intelligence is considered to be a *fixed* entity—a trait of the individual, like an object that is largely unmodifiable. We stress the term *object* (*res* in Latin) because the conceptualization of intelligence as an object is what turns it into something that can be measured, as though it is a steady state with fixed or static properties. If it is an object, it can be measured; it possesses a stable *quantity*, and this quantity can be measured.

REDEFINING THE NATURE OF INTELLIGENCE

In the surprisingly popular book *The Bell Curve* (it was on the best-seller list for many weeks in spite of its highly technical content), Herrnstein and Murray (1994) argued that intelligence is an object that exists in human beings in a certain quantity and with a certain quality, and that it is impossible to change it except to a minor degree (at most 10-15 percent). They were following up on the position of Arthur Jensen from the 1960s and others before him. This point of view, expressed in both academic and popular venues, offers various estimates with regard to the possible degree of change that can be attained, but these minor changes do not contradict the basic assumption, according to which intelligence is situated in the sphere of human beings' organic biological system and therefore cannot be modified. Again, the new neurosciences belie this position, as we will elaborate on in Chapter 14.

We maintain that there is no factor that determines the status of an individual as the IQ, and it is thus very important to have a functional definition of intelligence that reflects the adaptive potential of the human individual. One's IQ may determine what kind of occupation will be deemed suitable, what kind of wage one receives, the level and type of education that is accessible, and the type of society one will live in.

We define intelligence in an entirely different way—as a *force* that drives the organism to change itself and to change the structure of thinking and reaction in order to answer the needs that appear before it and change before its eyes. Thus, our definition of intelligence is not an object or a stable *trait* of human beings, but rather a dynamic energetic agent or *state* that is unstable and responsive to the person's need to modify him- or herself in order to adapt to situations and cope with them successfully.

We cannot predict (in the sense of predetermine) the existence of this energetic force. A human being can change in all kinds of directions, and we shall never be able to know precisely to what extent the limits of ability and potential have been reached. Consequently, these forces can be increased, reinforced, or—alternatively—curbed or diminished. Its fate depends on varied external and internal factors, but it is responsive to these factors.

Conceptualizing intelligence as *energy* represents a dramatic change, the significance of which will become clear as we discuss the question: How do we modify intelligence? But at this point in our discussion, we reiterate that we are not dealing with an object with fixed measurements or characteristics that cannot be changed, but with an energy that, as such, is highly modifiable.

The Measurement of Intelligence

The problem of measurement needs clarification. For generations, intelligence has been measured and quantified. There is nothing essentially wrong with this as long as it is understood that the results of such measurement are not static. A result obtained today may be totally different a year from now. Binet and Simon (1905), two pioneer French researchers who contributed greatly to the measurement of intelligence, wanted to help by classifying children in France for placement into regular and special educational frameworks. To this end they invented a test designed to define the abilities of children (the Binet-Simon Test), but they believed that these abilities were modifiable, and so they did not consider the results of their test to be the final word. On the other hand, those who came after Binet and Simon, particularly American adaptors such as Goddard and Terman, sought to turn psychology into an exact science and altered—unfortunately—the principles that Binet and Simon had established. Intelligence came to be viewed as having a final, irreversible nature—in structural and quantitative aspects. In so doing, they turned intelligence into a factor that cannot be changed. In their ardor to measure intelligence in a scientific way they made it completely rigid. Thus, paradoxically, we are much closer to Binet and Simon when we emphasize the dynamic quality of intelligence, referring to it—as we described earlier—as an energy rather than an object. From this alternative point of view, intelligence and its related cognitive processes are considered as reflecting a changeable state of the individual and not a fixed and immutable trait.

How to Achieve Structural Changes

The most difficult questions, which require an extensive discussion to answer, are:

- *What* is it that turns a student or any human being into the possessor of such a powerful capability for change as we maintain?

- *Where* does the uniqueness of a human being reside, and how does that uniqueness affect the capacity to change?
- *In what ways* is a human being different from other creatures, in whom the capacity to change is related to this uniqueness?
- *Why* do animals undergo such minimal evolutionary changes as compared to those that occur in a human being?
- *Do* the differences derive from biological characteristics or from additional causes and variables?

The Triple Ontology of Development

We can begin to consider these questions by examining the general course of human development. We have adapted a conceptualization of the French thinker Rom Harre, who proposed two major sources of development (a double ontology)—the *biological* and the *social* (Harre & Van Langen Rove, 1991). From the biological standpoint, the developing human being is a kind of community of cells that have coalesced and function together in a very organized, planned, and coordinated manner. This is the biogenetic individuality of the individual, who functions in interaction with the environment, takes from it what is required for existence, and that is all. There is also the sociocultural ontology, according to which human beings are the creation of society and are an outcome of interaction with the social environment, with cultural systems, and with means that only society can create.

The sociocultural ontology supplies us with a more observable answer to the questions regarding the sources that make a human being a modifiable creature. We maintain that a human being is the only creature in our world who is granted a special kind of connection with the world through human mediators. These vital people transmit the social mores and cultural treasures that have accumulated over thousands of years, generation after generation. These mediators enrich human beings not only with knowledge but also with thinking structures. This unique interaction among human beings occurs naturally in the course of development, but not always (if human development is subject to disruption, as in the Holocaust, for example).

We thus come to the third ontology—the necessary contribution to development through *mediated learning experience* (MLE). We have come to consider MLE is an essential aspect of human development, particularly as it may not occur sufficiently in situations of direct exposure to stimuli and experiences in the world—the biological and the sociocultural. It is needed to add to direct experience and to fully materialize human development. Human beings who do not receive sufficient MLE through the course of their development are deprived of essential aspects of developmental experience. MLE is used intergenerationally, from parent to child, from grandparent to grandchild, and within the family system (sibling to sibling), to enrich and intensify sociocultural experience. It is used voluntarily and consciously, in a goal-directed and reciprocal manner. We contend that this ontogeny is especially important in situations where individuals need more exposure and focusing that may be—or have been—available to them in their life experiences.

WHAT MAKES US MODIFIABLE?

When we ask what makes a human into a modifiable being, we now have an answer—modifiability is imparted to a human being by virtue of the mediation through which the world is mediated to him or her and creates tools and the preconditions necessary to become modified. From this standpoint, a human being is a unique creature. Although there are indications of mediation also in the animal world, they do not enable animals to transmit their experience to their descendants. Animals are limited in their ability to transmit their experience because they lack transmission tools. Did you ever see proof of the existence of an animal that lived in the past, apart from his physical testimony? We find traces of dinosaurs, for example, and their bones, but did they tell how they were made extinct? Human beings are the only ones who transmit their culture, and by the transmission of culture we mean not only transmission of information but formulation of experience so that succeeding generations can derive from them the means of adaptation to changes.

What causes a human being, in contrast to all other living creatures, to be prepared and even to wish to mediate for the next generation? We contend that in human beings there exists a need to mediate, created as a result of the awareness of death—one's sense of a finite existence. As the only creature conscious of the physical limitations of his or her biological life, human beings try to continue their personal existence beyond their physical limitations by transmitting their culture, their spiritual aspirations, and their experience to the generations that come after them.

It is this need for and quality of mediation, expressed through the provision of mediated learning experience (MLE), that will occupy us throughout the remainder of this volume. We will see how it is conceptualized and then applied in very direct and systematic ways to modify student functioning—often in the face of significant obstacles.

CHAPTER 4

Modifying Intelligence

Thus far we have raised three basic questions. The first is the question of the importance of intelligence, which represents all the cognitive aspects of our behavior. The second question deals with the possibility of modifying intelligence. Finally, the third question addresses the preferred ways the desired modification can be produced.

We answered the first question, hopefully convincingly, that intelligence is so important that we would wish to intervene to modify it, and we explained its importance through its being the force and the inclination existing in us to modify ourselves to adapt to new situations.

Now we address the second question and maintain that intelligence *is* modifiable. In fact, there is ever-increasing evidence that intelligence (as well as other human states and the neurophysiological structures in the brain) is clearly modifiable, despite its having a long and well-articulated history of being considered as innate and possessing important hereditary components. To reiterate our earlier arguments in this regard, we do not reject the hereditary components but consider them as not having the last and final word.

We are encouraged that perceptions regarding the nature of the biological factors and contributions have changed. Biologists and neurologists are presenting amazing data regarding the plasticity of the nervous system. Each day new research comes to light showing the flexibility and adaptability of the neural structure. It appears that even the chromosomal elements that were considered to be the stronghold of heredity are changing significantly, and that there occurs between them interaction that is liable to be very significant from the standpoint of the modification processes.

We now move to the position that sociocultural interaction is capable of causing a significant structural modification in the human being through the provision of mediated learning experience (MLE), even when the basis is biological-genetic and chromosomal. That is to say, we do not mean simply a quantitative change, or some behavioral additions, but a modification of the very structures responsible for the functioning of human beings.

YET RESISTANCE REMAINS!

We cannot, however, ignore resistance to this point of view. For example, Reuven Feuerstein presented to an audience of behavioral scientists the results of a project that we conducted among a population of very low-functioning children. To his joy, quite a few people in the audience had a close acquaintance with our project, had seen the children and their achievements, and supported his findings. However, one of the listeners stood up and argued: "Either the initial condition of those children was not as bad as you describe, or else their current state is not so good," meaning that he rejected outright the possibility of modification because he accepted the basic assumption that a human being is not modifiable. To a large extent, this assumption blocks the use of education as an instrument of modifying intervention. Unfortunately, this is consistent with those psychologists who argue that education helps those who have the hereditary and genetic tools that enable them to use the means that education provides, but is of little assistance for those who lack the innate skills required in order to produce significant learning.

This general outlook finds expression in many forms (we referred to *The Bell Curve* and what preceded it in the last chapter). The basic position of this line of thinking is that if a population lacks the appropriate hereditary conditions (as was presumed in certain specific racial and ethnic groups), its members will not be amenable to modifiability. It is, for example, maintained in several instances of respected publications that African Americans in the United States will never change because their intelligence is lower by approximately one standard deviation than that of the White population. Therefore, without reference to their status, their economic situation, or the educational and environmental conditions to which they have been exposed, the presumed intelligence and level of functioning of African Americans will always remain lower than that of the members of other racial/ethnic groups. This is an erroneous and damaging assumption about population groups that have been deprived of access and opportunities that are available to other groups. The primary damage is that such a position minimizes the reasons (and need) to find ways to deal with the educational and other potential interventions that could be employed. The tendency to use static approaches—to consider emotional, affective/energetic factors as more important aspects than intelligence, or to use behavioral approaches, according to which the behaviors and outcomes are the deciding aspects of intelligence—is derived from the assertion that, in any case, it is impossible to modify the intelligence. Therefore there is no point in dealing with it too much.

THE ARGUMENT IN SUPPORT OF MODIFIABILITY

We have a great deal of empirical data about individuals and groups who were at very low levels of functioning (i.e., with IQs in the 40–70 range) but were treated by us and achieved significant progress and normal functioning. Many even attained high levels of functioning after they had undergone our intervention program—the Feuerstein Instrumental Enrichment (FIE) Program that we will discuss in Chapter 11.

We also have data about modifiability in a chromosomally affected population. For instance, we treated children with Down syndrome who were considered to have a very low level of intelligence, in the IQ range of 30 to 70 at most. We proved that they were significantly modifiable in all areas that were generally considered to be beyond the bounds of their ability. However, this required great effort, because children with Down syndrome are not like other children—they need special, intense, and systematic mediation between themselves and the world for them to learn and progress. But the moment they receive it, we discern changes and the emergence of thinking structures that subsequently enable the attainment of much higher achievements than those that we, or others, deemed possible. Consequently, even the chromosome does not represent an insurmountable obstacle, and this also applies to different types of chromosomal deviations with their attendant cognitive and behavioral effects.

WORKING TO PRODUCE MODIFIABILITY

Now we come to a difficult question: How is it possible to realize the modifiability that, according to our assumption, exists in every human being?

The answer to this question leads us to the main pillar of the theory of structural cognitive modifiability (SCM): the theory and application of mediated learning experience (MLE), which will occupy us in the following three chapters and accompany us in all the other topics that we shall be dealing with in this book. As we have described above, MLE is one of the essential forms through which the human organism achieves interaction with the world—and what we defined in Chapter 3 as one of the basic sources of cognitive development. The human organism (and other animal species) maintains a direct interaction with the world, through direct exposure to stimuli. The organism (both human and lower animal species) learns through direct experience when nothing stands between it and the stimulus. For example, I take a cup that I have never seen before, turn it over, and the water in the cup pours out. I learn from this not to overturn the cup if I don't wish the water to pour out of it.

Thus a large part of our learning (and of the learning of other animals) occurs through direct experience—we hear voices, we see sights, and we absorb them, recognize them, and are potentially modified by exposure to them. The organism is modified (experientially and structurally) in the course of the learning process—after I have seen an object for the first time and know it, on my second encounter I shall identify it at once, because I have been exposed to it.

Learning through direct experience is, actually, the most common form of learning for every living organism, including human beings. However, direct exposure does not fully explain the potential for modifiability. In our view, the explanation for modifiability does not reside in direct experience, but in the potential for indirect learning. Mediated learning experience is what gives human beings the ability to modify themselves and the tools for learning that will enable the benefits of direct exposure to the world of stimuli.

MLE occurs when a person (mediator) who possesses knowledge, experience, and intentions mediates the world, makes it more understandable, and imparts meaning to it by adding to the direct stimuli. This will take many forms, but can be generalized to describe (to one degree or another) aspects of the human experience that it has accumulated over the years, and not just the immediate experience of the moment.

The relationship between direct learning and MLE can be formulated in this way: the more experience a person has had of exposure to mediated learning, the more he or she will derive benefit from direct exposure to the world. Conversely, the less a person experiences mediated learning, the more the influence and impact of direct learning will be decreased.

In this sense, mediated learning experience is altogether different from learning through direct exposure to stimuli, and this difference explains, to a large extent, the difference between human beings and other creatures. We elaborate on this concept in Chapter 5.

Mediating the Learning Experience

Mediated learning experience (MLE) is different from learning through direct exposure to stimuli. To illustrate this argument, we invite you to join us in a tour of a science museum, a tour that is rather exceptional because during it we shall not be looking at the exhibits but at the visitors. Reuven Feuerstein made the original tour with the late Professor Frank Oppenheimer, who founded the Exploratorium in San Francisco. Oppenheimer built it according to the didactic principle whereby it is sufficient for a human being to be in direct sensory contact with stimuli—visually and tactilely—to learn and become modified. Feuerstein's position, expressed to Oppenheimer in the course of the tour and discussed in more detail later on in this and following chapters, is different: To derive benefit from experiences a human mediator is required who will mediate the stimuli to the learner.

DIFFERENTIATING DIRECT LEARNING EXPERIENCE FROM MEDIATED LEARNING EXPERIENCE

To start with, let us observe Allan and his mother; afterward, we shall join William and his family.

> Allan walks around the big hall of the science museum. He runs from one exhibit to another, presses, moves, touches, pulls, looks, and runs again. His mother has long since stopped running after him. She hears his loud cries and is happy to see her son occupied with the world that unfolds before him and enthused by it. Once or twice she attempts to explain to Allan what is happening in front of him—how the ring was drawn to the magnet, for example—but he is far more interested in creating events rather than in understanding them.
>
> If we draw nearer to Allan and observe his activity, we shall very soon notice that his interaction with the exhibits is confined to sensory-physical activity only, whereas his thinking functions, necessary for comprehending the exhibits, are practically not involved. Even

though he appears busy, apparently (also cognitively), and very interested, if we were to draw near to him we would understand that his attention focuses on some exhibit only for a moment, when he presses its operating button, and before he even sees the results of pressing the button he moves on to another activity.

Allan activates the operating mechanism of an exhibit that demonstrates the interaction between two water containers. One can see that he doesn't understand that the rising of the surface of the water in one of the containers and not in the other results from the operating action that he produced. While he is still running here and there feverishly, Allan learns very little about the connection between his action and its outcome. Therefore, every action of his is as if he is doing it for the first time. He is behaving as if every moving object is there in order to be touched, pushed, and kicked, but not beyond that.

Allan experienced, apparently, what is generally termed "direct learning experience." Experience there most certainly was, but did learning also occur? It would seem not.

Allan's mother hoped, just as many parents and educators hope, that her son's direct interaction with the exhibits in the museum would cause him to learn operating principles and characteristics of the phenomena exposed to him. But it appears that looking and operating are not sufficient for learning. To understand what affected the waterline in the vessel, the ability to compare two consecutive situations is required, like the situation of the waterline in the vessel before the operation of the lever and the resulting change in the waterline. However, if Allan does not notice what happened he will be unable to learn about the relationship between the action and its results, and certainly not in that specific experience. Possibly, he will never know how to reproduce the event by repetition of the same action.

As we have said, Allan's mother is not alone in believing in the power of learning from direct experience. We should remind you that there exist three basic conceptions regarding the way in which the interaction with the environment leads to the development of thinking, to the development of the intelligence, and to the advancement of human beings.

Describing the Models for Learning

First is the behaviorist conception, according to which exposure to stimuli (S) causes change by inducing the person to make a response (R) to the stimulus. Piaget added the organism (O) to the equation—its characteristics, age, and stages of development as a function of processes of maturation—to explain not only the manner of the organism's response but also which of the stimuli it is exposed to are significant for it and which are not. This introduces the structural component. The question becomes, when does the stimulus become a source for learning, and in what way does the exposure to stimuli modify a human being's system of behavioral and thinking schemata?

The two approaches—the "stimulus-response (S-R)" model and the "stimulus-organism-response (S-O-R)" model—both assume that it is enough for a person to be in a kind of dialogue with the world, nature, and the surrounding stimuli in order to experience cognitive and intellective development. According to Piaget, the only requirement is for the organism to be at a certain level of maturity, to have reached a particular stage of development, and to be engaged in an active interaction with the world. That is to say, the organism must not only be exposed to the stimuli, but also must respond to them in a certain way in order for its thinking schemata (structures) to develop and pass (using Piaget's terminology) from the sensory-motor stage to the operational-concrete stage, and afterward to the formal operational logic stage.

In these two approaches, there is no reference to the role of the human factor in this developmental process as a bearer of the human culture that has accumulated over thousands of generations and as its transmitter. What mediates the world for human beings and enables them to absorb it through the actions of the mediator is not taken into account. Those who hold to these approaches do not perceive the human mediator as having a crucial influence on a human being's development and, in the final analysis, as being the precipitator of the change. Herein lies the great difference between these two approaches and the third approach, according to which the person who mediates is not an object that the child meets and learns from by chance, as one also learns from an encounter with a tree, a bird, or a glass of water. The individual learns from the human mediator the objects and nature in themselves that do not and cannot purposively or intentionally mediate. The human mediator is the transmitter of the wider cultural and meaningful elements of the objects and events of direct experience. This is the foundation of a wide range of parental- and teacher-oriented interventions, engaging the mediators in adaptive, creative, and innovative activities.

Constructing the MLE Model

According to our approach, we add the human being to the S-O-R schemata and place an "H" for the human mediator between the stimulus and the organism and between the organism and response, as seen in Figure 5.1.

The human mediator does not continually or constantly impose on the person being mediated and the world. He or she does not cover all the territory between them but leaves the mediatee a big area of direct exposure to stimuli. But in the area in which the mediating agent engages, the mediator is active in a number of ways. An example is the significant modification of the stimulus and a focused exposure to the mediatee in a systematic, intentional, and controlled manner. Thereby, the mediator imparts to the mediatee the components that will be responsible for his or her ability to understand phenomena, to look among them for associations and connections, and thereby to derive benefit from them and be modified.

Figure 5.1. Model of Mediated Learning Experience

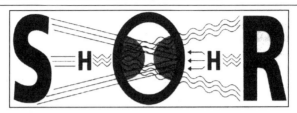

Before we go further into the depths of MLE theory, let us return to our museum tour:

> On seeing Allan's obvious enjoyment, I asked myself whether one ought to disturb that enjoyment. Are we not liable to drive away Allan's wonderful spontaneity if we force upon him an artificial state of learning? Will we not harm the experience of discovery if we position ourselves between Allan and the world of stimuli surrounding him?

Many educators have long believed that such enforcement is not only unnecessary, but also undesirable and even damaging to a child's personality, his or her independence, and his or her sense of freedom.

Traces of this point of view regarding thinking can be found in Jean-Jacques Rousseau's belief that nature does a perfect job and that, when adults try to teach a child, they only succeed in confusing or even corrupting him or her. Those who hold to this and other similar views assume that direct exposure to a stimulus without any learning mediation (by an intentional and engaged mediator) will lead to the appropriate cognitive behavior, as a part of the natural development and growth process. We question the logic behind a sole reliance on the direct learning approach because of the way in which children develop and the repertoire of the behaviors that build intelligence (as we believe it should be defined—see our discussion in Chapter 3).

But let us return to Allan:

> Now and again, tired from his travels, Allan returns to his mother. She bestows a broad smile on him and a warm hug, and asks him if he liked what he had seen and done. Adam answers with a stream of superlatives. "I really love the things here very much. They are wonderful!" The mother asks him if he wants to go and see them again. "Yes!!" he replies.
>
> The mother does not try at all to elicit from the boy a more discerning description about what he has seen, to discover why the things interested him, or if he had identified the principle governing the transfer of the water from one container to another.

In describing his enthusiastic impressions of the museum, Allan accompanies his explanations with cries and sounds and gestures to illustrate some of the outstanding exhibits he had seen. The movement of the steam engine pistons had captivated him in particular, although he described the revolutions of the engine with characteristic movements (of recurring broad revolutions of his hands and arms); he only expressed his enjoyment thereby. He didn't ask: "What causes the pistons' movements?" "Why do they revolve?" Nor did his mother ask him these questions. She contented herself with the answers that he gave.

Before we examine the alternative to the direct learning approach, we shall describe another child, William, who also came to look at the exhibits in that same science museum:

William, a little younger than Allan, was in the company of Sara, his sister, and his mother who was carrying his one-year-old brother on her back. The group proceeded from exhibit to exhibit in a completely different way to that of Allan and his mother. In contrast to Allan, who flitted from one exhibit to another like a butterfly, unpredictably, William and his family progressed in a very organized manner. It was easy to follow the planned and directed character of their route, with the aid of William's directing finger and his sister's signals as to when to go on to the next exhibit, and which one to stop at for a more thorough investigation. When they decided where to spend their time, an entire range of organization and distribution of activities governed their interaction with the exhibit: the family stopped in front of one exhibit that had earlier attracted their attention. The sign above it invited them to make bubbles from a big cup of liquid soap.

William and Sara were really excited. They worked in cooperation, one of them filling a spoon with soap and the second one blowing onto it and making the bubbles. Their mother stood beside them, instructing them where to blow, and demonstrating to them how to regulate the stream of air. She interpreted their success as a sign of their ability and as a result of the cooperation between them. When they came to the two interconnected water containers seen in Figure 5.2 (the same exhibit that had also interested Allan), the mother stationed herself, together with Sara, to the left of the system, and William stood to its right. What followed was a wonderfully coordinated interactive relationship. The mother began by drawing her children's attention to the colored waterline in each of the containers. Afterward, Sara turned the left lever, thus causing the waterline on the right to drop, and immediately after her William turned the right-hand lever, causing the waterline in the left-hand container to drop. Noting the changes caused in each of the containers, the mother suggested that they let go of the levers and try to anticipate what would happen the moment the levers returned to their resting state!

Figure 5.2. The Mechanism of the Connected Containers

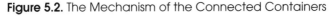

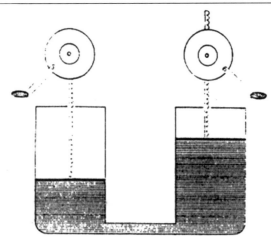

The mother mediated to the children a mental operation of anticipation (that is to say, anticipating the answer mentally and afterward checking whether it had actually occurred).

The children don't answer straight away. Their mother urges them: "Think, please." William estimates that the water will flow into the container on his side, but is unable to give a reason for his answer (Sara continues to stare at the containers in the hope that something will happen).

Their mother hints: "Do you remember what the height of the water was before you turned the lever?" Now the two children grasp what the answer is: The water will return to its previous position before they activated the levers. Even the baby, perched on the mother's back, follows her indicating fingers with its gaze.

What did the mother intend by these acts? What did she intend by her intervention? We were, of course, unable to read her thoughts. One might conclude through reflection on her actions that her behavior was intentional: She wanted her children to discover the way in which the interconnected containers worked. Because she understood that she had to create the conceptual and cognitive conditions necessary for this discovery to occur, she focused her children's attention on the levers, on the features of the containers, and on the height of the water in each of them. By describing everything in detail, she turned a focus on the parts into a means whereby the children understood the action of the exhibit's mechanism: The mother drew the children's attention to the changes that were produced in sequence by each of them. She caused them to remember what the waterline had been before they had acted and asked them to anticipate: "What would happen if the movement was stopped?" When the children hesitated, the mother didn't jump in with the ready answer as parents sometimes are tempted to do. On the contrary, she gave them time to think, and when she felt they needed assistance, she suggested to them to compare the current height of the water with its initial height, and in this way she hinted to them to connect the two sources of information required to discover the principle behind what they had seen.

How different was the quality of the interaction in the two cases? Did William grasp more than Allan? In terms of sensory absorption, there was no apparent difference between them. Did Allan do less? Definitely not! Allan was far more active than William and managed to "cover," by running around, a greater exhibition area. However, because nobody had prevented Allan from submitting to the drawing power of each exhibit, and his need to experience innovations, his experience was superficial. His moving and manipulating the exhibits, in themselves, did not cause him to reflect on what was happening in the exhibit, and therefore he didn't understand the connection between his actions and what happened.

What caused the two boys to function so differently when exposed to the same kind of stimulus? In our opinion, the difference lies in the nature of their interaction with the world: William experienced interaction of a mediated learning nature, whereas Allan experienced direct, unmediated interaction.

Allan was exposed to a stimulus (S) and reacted (R) in ways that the stimulus enabled or even encouraged. This exposure, and the boy's reaction to it, is considered from the perspective of learning experts with a behaviorist approach a sufficient condition for the boy's cognitive development in many areas. A chain of stimuli and reactions is considered, in the view of those same experts, as a sufficient source for learning, especially when there are clear outcomes to the child's behavior. In relating to the outcomes of the behavior, the child builds associations between the S and R, and these associations serve as sources of reinforcement of the behavior. Such a scenario can occur in two directions—avoiding a repetition of a behavior whose outcomes were found to be undesirable, or repeating a behavior whose outcomes were found desirable. According to this learning model, certain behaviors become, in the end, a part of the individual's repertoire of behaviors.

However, is this really how learning occurs? In our description of Allan's responses to the museum, after repeated interactions with the exhibits, Allan was unable to point to the lever that had caused the machine to move in one direction or another, or even to the one that had caused it to move or to stop. This inability was due to the fact that when he turned the lever/handle, he did not pay attention to the changes in the position of the lever.

He did not notice the difference between the first lever and the second lever or between what happened when he turned one lever and didn't turn the second one. He did not analyze the source or outcomes of his actions, and thus did not develop any insights or structural knowledge from his extensive direct experiences.

Repeated actions, unaccompanied by thinking and understanding processes, may perhaps cause enjoyment and reinforcement but do not necessarily produce learning. By activating a strategy of trial and error, Allan was forced to rediscover, at each action of the machine, which lever caused which reaction. Just like the fox in Aesop's fable, he emerged from the vineyard just as emaciated as he had entered it.

THE ROLE OF THE MEDIATOR
IN MEDIATED LEARNING EXPERIENCE

Allan's case demonstrates that in order to turn experience into learning, one must encourage the student to compare, collect, and classify data and to assign significance to the current experience in relation to previous experience.

This active method of experience in the world is a product of the form of interaction that is mediated learning experience (MLE). In a situation of mediated learning, the organism (O) being directly exposed to a stimulus (S) reacts and responds (R) with skill and completeness only after the characteristics of the stimulus have been sorted out, classified, differentiated, shaped and adapted, and organized by a mature human mediator (H).

That is to say, in a direct learning encounter, even when an adult teacher/parent is present, he/she is an object like any other object, even if he/she is a living and talking object who gives the child information that nature itself does not provide. It is not the adult's intention to mediate for the child, and even if it does occur, this intention does not in any way modify the type of the interaction between the child and the world.

But if the teaching adult is not a source for development of intelligence, how does it develop? Piaget maintained that every person who undergoes the initial development stages and reaches the stage of formal thinking should also attain high levels of thinking—including abstract and ethical thinking—through a combined process of gradually growing mental maturation and interaction with the environment to which one is directly exposed. When Piaget's tests are used to examine people who are supposed to be capable of high levels of thinking—university students, for example—we find that only 30-40% of them, at most, utilize formal thinking, whereas, according to Piaget, everyone should be able to attain it by themselves.

What then is the origin of the difference between human beings? Piaget came close to an answer when he added the "O" to the S-R paradigm. By doing so, he acknowledged that there is a central organizing entity—the organism—that undergoes a process of change through maturation, which enables a differential interaction with the stimuli and the results of behavioral responses. The organism in this conceptualization is able to detect and have access to an ever-wider range of stimuli and experiences. Should we relate it solely to biological or hereditary differences? Piaget didn't think so, but he was busy discovering the universal elements (or "laws") that govern a human being's development, and he wasn't interested in the differences between human beings.

We argue that in Piaget's approach there is no explanation either for the differences between people or for the process responsible for the coming into being of the cognitive functions that are activated in different situations. Therefore, from our point of view, Piaget's theory does not lead to real intervention. Also, for us, recent neurophysiological research points to the "O" as the brain, and its plasticity is determined by the interactions between the "S" and the "R" with the very necessary interventions from the "H"— the human mediator.

To better understand the nature of this distinction, we refer to the work of Hans Aebli, one of Piaget's outstanding pupils, who wrote a book about the psychological implications of teaching from the Piagetan perspective (Aebli, 1951). He argued that if we were to draw applicable conclusions from Piaget's theory, we shall have to say: "If the child/human being has reached the level of the thinking schemas he/she does not need learning any more, and if he hasn't done so—the learning will not help." Actually, this is not unlike the simple problem that confronted us when we worked with populations with normal mental functioning and ability, who for some reason didn't act like this in practice. We asked ourselves whether this was a genetic phenomenon or if it originated in the level of mediation that these people had received. We wondered whether they had received the mediation that would enable them to learn from their experience.

Analyzing Allan's and William's Learning Experience

To answer these questions, we shall compare the experiences of William and Allan, the children who visited the science museum: William's experience was substantially different from that of Allan. In the course of repeated encounters with the stimulus afforded by the exhibits, William was capable not only of working the machine and repeating its earlier outcome but could also anticipate how it would affect the outcomes if he changed the mode of operation.

William's mother, as a mediator, created in him what the encounter with the machine and its operation by themselves could never have produced: knowledge of and motivation to learn more about the relations between parts of events in which, in retrospect, could be found continuity, order, consistency, cause and effect, and so on.

It was the mother's mediating interaction that enabled William and his sister Sara to reach beyond getting to know the levers in the exhibit and to understand their functions and the way these functions were connected to other similar functions. The mediating interaction raised William's thinking ability to a level in which he was capable of deriving benefit from every task, making him more experienced, more interested, and more capable.

By positioning herself as a mediator between William and his responses, the mother established the pattern of his response—she received one answer and encouraged him to formulate other possible answers. When William, for example, used gestures to describe the connection between the turning of the lever and the change of height of the water, his mother encouraged him gently to answer with words. By contrast, Allan's mother did not station herself between her son and the stimulus, and did not encourage him to give verbal descriptions or to improve his answers. Despite the fact that Allan's exposure to the stimuli in the museum was for him an exciting experience, which influenced his motivation in general (he wanted to return to the museum), he did not appear to derive much cognitive benefit from it, as evidenced by the low level of his capability when he performed the tasks.

The lack of mediated learning experiences is liable, therefore, to cause a person to derive very little from a direct encounter with learning tasks. One's adjustment ability will be extremely weak and will be expressed by a lack of flexibility when having to adapt to new and complex situations.

Further Examples of the Effects of Mediated Learning Experience

Following Piaget's lead, Reuven Feuerstein conducted an experiment with thousands of children and youngsters in grades 3 to 8 that highlighted the power of mediated learning experience.

These are the stages of the experiment illustrated in Figure 5.3:

1. The examinees are shown a square bottle that is half-filled with blue water.
2. The bottle is covered by a cloth. The bottle's position is changed in front of the examinees, and a strip of paper is placed in front of the examinees with drawings of the bottle when it is tilted in different directions, simultaneously with the positions of the bottle in the hands of the examiner. The examinees are asked to predict how the waterline will look in the turned-over bottle.
3. The bottle is uncovered again, and the examinees are asked to draw the waterline according to every position that the examiner sets the bottle in. At this stage, direct learning supposedly takes place.
4. The bottle is covered again and the nature of the learning is examined. The process is repeated fully with a round bottle in order to examine the quality of the learning that has taken place, from the standpoint of its resistance to change.

Figure 5.3 The Experiment of the Tilted Bottles

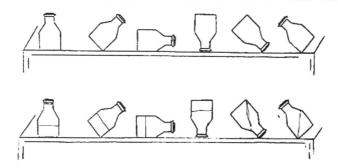

In the first row of the diagram the bottle is drawn as it stands in various tilted positions. In the second row, the waterline in the bottle is also drawn.

We examined different populations and found that at the lower elementary level, even high-performing children tended to make errors and "to stick" the water at the bottom of the bottle without noticing its tilt or taking into account the influence of gravity. However, the most interesting finding was that in the answers of the examinees after the stage of experience and learning, we found a difference between children who had been given mediation and who came from homes where the encounters with nature were accompanied by explanations, formulations, and varied interventions and those children who had not received the same level of mediation.

When children who had received mediation were confronted for the first time by the dilemma concerning the position of the water in the bottle, even though they were mistaken like the other children, they learned from the exposure to the stimulus and corrected themselves in the course of the experiment. On the other hand, those who had not had mediation, although they had seen the bottles in the experiment and had used bottles all of their lives—and had drunk water from cups, and knew that if the cup is tilted it can be drunk from—they had not learned how to use their direct experiences to draw the conclusion that the water always remains in a horizontal state, without relation to the position of the container it is in.

The findings were clear and recurred when this test was administered among thousands of children.

We maintain, therefore, that dialogue with nature, even if it is very active, is not sufficient to create in a human being the changes that will enable an adaptation to new situations. Mediated learning, on the other hand, offers an interactive quality vouchsafed only to human beings and that is responsible for their unique modifiability. The mediator turns every event and every experience into an opportunity for change and for expanding the schemata of the activity for the recipient of the mediation. This special interaction occurs in the course of the use of different and varied forms of communication, and increases the person's ability to derive benefit also from interaction that is created by unmediated (direct) exposure to stimuli.

SUMMING UP

We shall sum up this chapter by stressing the unique characteristics of the mediated interaction: The mediated interaction introduces order into a human being's encounter with the world. An outstanding characteristic of the direct exposure of a person to stimuli is the randomness and unpredictability of the encounter. Not only does the stimulus not always appear, but the person is not always in a state of readiness to absorb it. Possibly, the human being apprehended the stimulus when it arrived, or perhaps not! That is to say, a person's chance encounter with stimuli cannot guarantee that he/she will always and unavoidably derive benefit from their appearance and from the interaction with them. This is not the case in the situation where the mediator is stationed between the stimulus and the person, as if saying:

> I want you to see this particular stimulus; I want you to see it in this situation. I shall do everything to make it possible; I shall even change the stimulus for it to attract your gaze, even if you are not interested in seeing it. Before you see it, I shall make sure that you see something else for you to identify the connection between what you are seeing now and what came before it or what will come after it.

The mediator introduces order into this world of stimuli that is liable, in itself, to be very random. The order will enable the recipient of the mediation to discover associations between the stimuli by making comparisons and other mental operations.

The mediating interaction gives human beings tools for reflecting on phenomena and understanding the connections between them, as well as for discovering the system of laws governing them. For example, many children and quite a few adults don't understand the principle according to which the moon's appearances change—why it waxes and wanes, and when and why it appears full during the month. That is to say, the fact that we see the moon every evening does not induce us to gaze at it in order to understand the laws governing its phases. Think about all those discoveries which today we take for granted—discoveries that are the result of thousands of years of contemplation that not only transmitted knowledge and data to us but also taught us how to reflect.

Mediated learning is the most outstanding expression of the significance of human culture, which transmits to the student not only quantities of knowledge and skills, but also (and mainly) ways of reflecting on phenomena and ways to look for connections between them. Human culture transmits, in addition to historical contents, that which lies outside the person's direct sensory perception, the desire to search for and discover systems of laws and to try to verify or reject them with subsequent experiences. That is to say, beyond the knowledge that a person would not obtain were it not for his having a mediator. Furthermore, without a mediator, even if one did obtain it, one would not understand its significance. The mediator creates in a person an approach, a form of reference, a desire to understand phenomena, a need to find order in them, to understand the order that is revealed, and to create it for oneself. In this way, mediation increases the person's ability to derive benefit from the direct exposure to stimuli.

IS MLE UNIQUE TO THE HUMAN RACE?

There exists evidence that when mediation is given to certain types of primates, previously nonexistent functions are created in them. A wonderful example is the work of Patterson (1978, 1981) with Koko, a female orangutan. Through her interactions with Dr. Patterson, Koko learned American Sign Language (ASL), acquired a very large vocabulary, and also learned several swear words and even to tell lies and jokes. According to Patterson's description, her work with Koko corresponds with the MLE model largely because of the parameters that characterize this interactive quality. Furthermore, she reported that when Koko got to know Mickey, a young male orangutan, Koko began to mediate to Mickey what she had learned from Dr. Patterson. In both of these primates and in other research with chimpanzees, we see a kind of mediation that would not exist had not a human factor introduced this kind of interaction with the environment into their world. The changes were most certainly significant.

In a similar vein, Professor Jerome Bruner, the well-known developmental psychologist, commented when he heard Reuven Feuerstein describing the theory of MLE: "MLE is not only designed for the handicapped, it is designed for all of us, since it is what makes us human."

The theory of mediated learning experience will continue to preoccupy us in subsequent chapters of this book because it is the main pillar of the theory and practice of structural cognitive modifiability (SCM). In summary, MLE has two main functions:

- It explains students' and all human beings' ability to modify themselves, which we are all witness to, even though we sometimes deny it unjustifiably.
- It enables increasing the modifiability of students in circumstances where, for various reasons, such modifiability is weak or does not exist.

CHAPTER 6

Creating the Conditions for Successful Learning: The Mediated Learning Experience (MLE)

The experience of mediation is a form of interaction that accompanies human beings' development and has shaped human experience (developmental and cultural) long before the formulation of the theory of mediated learning experience (MLE). Professor Feuerstein frequently recalls how his mother, of blessed memory, mediated the world to him long before he began to formulate this concept. He reflects "actually, a large part of what I know today about mediation I learned from her, and I am far from unique in this regard." To learn what mediation is, we must go to the mothers who have been mediating to their children since the coming of human existence—to observe them and to understand their actions.

Professor James Comer is a psychiatrist, seminal educator, and member of the faculty of Yale University. His work has focused on the education of African American children (he is African American). He commented after attending one of my lectures about MLE:

> Everything that is in me today I learned to be from the mediation which my mother gave me, when she instructed me how to clean the homes of the white people she worked for—how to remove the dust from every corner. Her mediation is what enabled me to achieve all that I do today as a psychiatrist.

In his own words, he expressed an important characteristic of the quality of the mediated interaction: mediation is not necessarily verbal or language dependent. It is, however, certainly *intentional*—that is, the mediator wants it to happen and does things to bring it to the mediatee. It begins, basically, from the first day of the baby's life, when the mother looks the infant straight in the eye and tries to catch its gaze. The baby also begins to focus on the mother's face very soon after birth, trying to observe the changes that take place in it and reacting to them.

 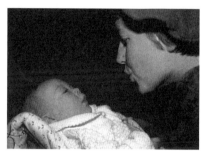

At the top of this page, we include a sequence of photographs showing a grandfather (the senior author) and mother mediating to a young infant and illustrating the readiness to respond to mediated imitation at an early age. The importance of this interaction is that all children have a potential to register and respond at much earlier ages than usually presumed. For children with special needs, such as those with Down syndrome, this early mediated imitation is vital to the development of further abilities that are well within the children's behavioral repertoires if early and systematic stimulation is offered. At this stage the infant usually prefers the mother over the father and others because the mother is the most significant figure. The infant gradually but rapidly learns to distinguish between significant figures and less-significant ones in its immediate experience. When I, as a stranger, try to catch the baby's gaze, its eyes dart from me, and I have to perform all manner of manipulations to catch its gaze. On the other hand, when only the mother is present in the vicinity, the baby is likely to completely turn its body to capture her gaze. The mother gives the baby preverbal mediation, which includes mediation for imitation, mediation for looking for that which has vanished from the field of vision, and for additional behavioral systems that are preverbal in character, even though they are accompanied verbally.

This type of mediation, which the mother gives her child at the start of its way in the world, influences the form of interaction that the child creates with the environment. The child learns to select (and search for) the objects that will be focused on (visually) for a longer period. MLE does not depend on the language in which the interaction occurs. All modalities of the interaction bear within them qualities of mediated learning; gestural and physical interaction, exposure to models of behavioral imitation, and—of course—verbal interaction, which is of special significance and quality due to its capacity to expand and elaborate the other modalities of MLE. We have recently completed a small guidebook for the mediation of early language development—*Mediated Soliloquy: Theory, Concept, and a Guide to Practical Applications* (in press).

A child who watches its father's actions—cutting a tree to make it into a canoe, for example—also gains experience in mediated interaction: the father does not always explain his actions to the child verbally. He only invites the child to watch: "Stand here; see what I am doing." The father positions himself so that the child may see his actions, and the child learns the order of the actions leading to achieving the goal—made known to the child even though the canoe is not yet visible—of turning the tree trunk into a canoe. The father's intention to mediate is demonstrated in the manner in which he executes his actions and in the changes he introduces into those actions in order for them to be clearly visible, understood, and finally imitated by his child. The verbal interaction can be minimal, without necessarily diminishing its mediational value.

THE PARAMETERS OF
MEDIATED LEARNING EXPERIENCE

Mediated interaction is composed of two groups of parameters: the first group includes parameters that are responsible for the universal character of the phenomenon of human modifiability—for the plasticity that characterizes the human being. This group contains three parameters that create the essential conditions to transform an interaction into MLE. In other words, without them the interaction will not be mediational!

The second group of parameters includes those that direct the modifiability in different ways, depending on culture and interpersonal difference. These parameters are responsible for the differentiation of the mediated interaction (research has shown that even identical twins can receive completely different mediation from the same mother or respond differently to an identical mediation). We have called these parameters *situational* or *phase specific* because they do not occur in every interaction but are related to specific experiences, needs, and exposures of the learner.

In this chapter we shall characterize the three parameters belonging to the first group, and we shall devote the following chapter to the parameters of the mediated interaction.

As we learned from Allan, who was described in the last chapter, not every interaction between the mother and her child, between a teacher and a student, or between people in general reflects or contains the qualities of mediation. There are three essential characteristics that transform an interaction into MLE: *intentionality and reciprocity, transcendence,* and *the mediation of meaning.* Together, the three of these qualities create in the student the potential for structural modifiability, as an option common to all human beings, whether they possess different chromosomal organic structures, regardless of racial, ethnic, cultural, or socioeconomic differences.

We shall now describe each of these three parameters.

Intentionality and Reciprocity

In the mediated learning interaction, the specific content of the interaction, however important it may be, is shaped by the mediated intentionality.

- "I want you to listen to what I am saying. Therefore, I am saying it in a loud voice."
- "When I speak to you quietly, I have an intention. I want you to make an effort to listen, not only to hear."
- "I want you to know the order of the actions, therefore I repeat it many times."

I want the learning child—the child I mediate to—to recognize a particular object of focus—and not a different one—here and not in another place, now and not at another time. I include not only the material being learned but also the components of time, place, order, and organization, which are not necessarily or automatically perceived or attended to.

The mediator with intentionality changes the stimuli, causes them to be more salient, more powerful, more imposing, and ultimately more understandable and important to the recipient of the mediation (the mediatee/student). But simply changing the stimulus is not sufficient; the mediator also changes the recipient of the mediation—if the mediatee is drowsy, the mediator will induce a state of wakefulness. If the student responds slowly, the mediator will adjust the rate of the flow of the stimuli to the tempo of the mediatee so that they can be absorbed. However, if the skilled mediator observes that these interventions are not effective, the mediator will adapt his or her reactions, change him or herself, and modify the methods of the mediation in order to ensure that what is being conveyed will be absorbed by the student. That is to say, the intention to mediate modifies the three partners to the interaction—the mediator or mediating teacher, the world of stimuli, and the student. The mediation process can be likened to a loop, as shown in Figure 6.1.

Figure 6.1. The Mediational Loop

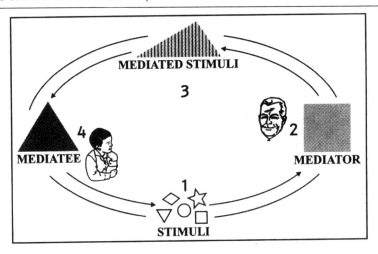

Let us analyze this schema to understand how it reflects the process of mediation. For the learner, there exists a collection of stimuli, represented in the diagram by a group of geometric forms. The mediator sorts the stimuli and chooses from them one stimulus to be focused on—separating/isolating one triangle from the group—enlarging it, changing its shape and color to make it more salient, elaborating or exaggerating its characteristics to make it meaningful, and presenting it to the mediatee in order to facilitate its reception. The mediatee or student absorbs the mediated triangle according to the aspects that have been the focus of the mediation, and, when it is returned to the stimulus array, it will be known, understood, remembered, structurally assimilated, and thus responded to meaningfully in subsequent encounters, despite any changes in its direct and particular characteristics—dimensions, color, geometric properties, and so on. Why choose the triangle? That simply is a metaphor for some aspect of the stimulus world that the mediator deems important to emphasize, according to the mediator's analysis of the needs of the learner or the demands of the environment.

The mediational loop is closed (that is to say, it becomes a loop) only if the message regarding the stimulus passes from the mediator to the mediatee, is absorbed and registered, and leads to a process of generalization, conservation of the object, and ultimately abstract thinking. When I mediate my intention to a child—why I chose this stimulus, why I chose to emphasize this principle and not another, and why I chose this method and not another (which can also be conveyed to and understood by very young children)—I give the child the means of mediating to him- or herself when the mediator is no longer standing between him or her and the world—the quality of self-perpetuation of learning.

This is where reciprocity enters the picture, when the student or mediatee shares in the intention of the mediator and transforms the intention into an explicit, voluntary, and conscious act. To achieve reciprocity, I transfer to the mediatee my intentions, enabling the decision (willfully, consciously) of the mediatee to decide in which ways the reality that has been experienced will be responded to when the mediator is not present.

Intention and reciprocity breathe a new spirit of life into the interaction between the mediator and the mediatee. Every activity becomes an opportunity for mediation—from the simplest to the most complex—beginning with caring for the baby, imparting habits of cleanliness, imparting the ability to avoid life-threatening actions, orienting toward basic skills, and ending with teaching poetry, history, or philosophy—the process of mediation is experienced and needs to be experienced. These life-affirming interactions will receive a special character from the experience of mediated learning if they are intentionally designed, carried out in a systematic and empathic manner, and generate a reciprocal reaction.

However, intentionality alone is not sufficient. One can find intentionality among animals; we assume that the cat who takes her kittens out to the garden to show them how and where to eliminate and conceal their body wastes has an intention reflected in the way she waits before performing the act until the whole litter has drawn near and can observe her actions. That is to say, the intentionality exists, but it is connected with an activity that is based on the hereditary needs and inclinations of an animal that has to cover its tracks for fear of beasts of prey. With human beings, on the other hand, the mediation is characterized by the intention to go beyond the situation in which it was performed. This leads to the second universal quality of MLE.

Transcendence

In nature there is an essential movement requiring mediation toward goals that go beyond direct and immediate experience. Human existence requires an ultimate achievement of a distance from the object of an activity: the hunter acts within a relatively short distance from the necessary object of his or her intention, just like the cat that we described above. Farmers, on the other hand, act over a larger distance of time and space: they sow today to harvest the next year. Planting is done with the expectation that with the passage of time and occurrence of specific conditions, the desired outcome (the harvest) will be experienced.

The ability to act over increasingly large distances of time, space, and levels of abstraction is a main characteristic of human development. A human being uses the factors of time and space, and processes the world through them. This type of activity, which is distant from the objective, has created many changes in human beings: we must reject gratifications and we must distinguish between the goal and the actions required to achieve it. This distance demands of us our ability to represent our experience—we must imagine what will happen in another year if we do not invest in planting and sowing or, alternatively, what will happen if we do invest in them. Specifically, we must anticipate and ask ourselves "what will happen if we act differently, beyond our immediate needs?"

The relationship of a human being with the world is regulated by increasingly growing distances between the self and the objects of one's investment—between the inputs and the outcomes. Other living creatures do not create any kind of attitude to the world because there does not exist between them and the world the distance required for the development of relationships. For animals, their world is made up only of what suits their transient needs. They see in the world only what is near to them. In any case, the world of a human being is built increasingly and precisely when one finds oneself at a distance that will permit a dualism of man–world. Martin Buber made this distinction in his concepts of *urdestanz* and *underbeziehung*.

How do we foster the process of getting further away from the object of the activity and the immediate need? How do we create an attitude to the world that characterizes the student? How do we create the ability to transfer that which is learned to all areas of life? Our answer is that we create this through the mediation of transcendence. Thus, there is a special significance of transcendence—it is the humanizing factor of the interaction between a human being and the world.

We shall examine, for example, the mediating of transcendence given to children at mealtime:

> The main function of the interaction that occurs at mealtimes in a family is to ensure the physical survival of children by satisfying their needs. In order to achieve this aim, the location of the feeding is unimportant (whether on the table or under it), as is the manner of the feeding (with hands or with a knife and fork) or the order of the feeding. There is no need at all to impose on this interaction an order of time and place (apart from the time of the hunger), or to add to it the washing of the hands or a prayer. The interaction in itself does not require anything apart from the act of eating, which ensures the child's survival.

In this situation, the human mediator creates conditions that are not practical necessities but express a cultural need—the mediator transmits to the child the principle of "the culture of eating" that is the norm in their shared society. The culture transmits a set order of eating, a place where one eats, and times at which one eats. The attitude to food is a transition/elaboration from the function of the biological existence that it fulfills, and this attitude is transmitted by means of the mediation of transcendence.

The mediating of transcendence does not relate, therefore, simply to generalizations, conceptualizations, and abstract functions. Moreover, it is not even dependent on the explicit awareness of those involved in the mediated interaction (of either the mediator or the mediatee). The need to go outside and beyond the immediate situation of survival creates operative expressions and techniques that each and every culture uses in order to transmit itself to its future generations and thus ensure its continuity.

Through the mediating of transcendence, cultures go far beyond the individual, immediate, and physical needs of survival and attain the collective objectives of survival—objectives that at the group level are part of their spiritual collective. The transcendental component in mediated learning has extremely important functions: it creates in human beings a system of needs that are very distant from their primary needs. For example, knowing that pumpkins and marrows belong to the same vegetable family does not contribute anything at all to the act of eating them for the sake of physical survival. A person can benefit from eating them even without this knowledge—in fact, how many readers even know what a marrow is? But the mediated interaction that continues beyond the act of eating creates in human beings fresh needs—for example, to collect knowledge and to understand the world—and turns them into independent and extremely powerful needs. Differentiating pumpkins and marrows might inspire a person to learn more about varieties of vegetables, and so on. A group of students who were learning that female kangaroos have pouches and are members of the marsupial family were curious and did research on other marsupials that have pouches as well.

A person who goes without one's evening meal in order to go to a concert does not satisfy a need that one was born with. This is a product of a culture that was transmitted through mediation and creates new and different needs, and these needs are those that raise the level of the individual's existence to a higher level of a human being's potential development.

The mediating of transcendence creates in a human being a great diversity of possibilities of action and reaction, whose significance is the resulting flexibility and creativity of response, and which enables the propensity for a permanent modifiability to adapt to new situations.

As with so many other aspects of SCM and MLE, the findings of the new neurophysiology, particularly that of the mirror neurons, make the mechanism of transmission occurring in the mediation of transcendence more understandable from not only the cultural but also the neurological perspective.

The Mediation of Meaning

The third component, which is essential for the existence of interactions with a mediating value, is the mediation of meaning. The mediator is not content with transmitting content to the child, but must also be responsive to questions such as: "Why is this content important? Why must we learn it?"

In this way the mediator creates in the child an energetic capacity, which constitutes a motive for accepting and absorbing the mediation and using it. The mediation of meaning is what creates the motivational and emotional forces that drive our activity and our behavior. The mediation of meaning contributes to the quality and formative power of the interaction in two ways:

- Meaning makes the mediator's messages understandable and reasoned, also for extension and application beyond the immediate situation.
- It arouses the need of the recipient of the mediation to look for further and more personal meanings for oneself.

We shall examine the first contribution to meaning through a quite frequent example of interaction between a mother and her son:

> The mother, on seeing her son coming near to the fire, cries, "No!" We presume that the mother has created an interaction with meaning—she has prevented the child from approaching the fire and has saved his hand from being burned. But we ask: Is this an interaction with a mediational value? What remains to the child from his mother's cry that caused him to move his hand away from the fire? Will this cry cause him to avoid touching electricity? Will he also know to move away from other kinds of fire? Will he know how to distinguish between extending his hand dangerously and doing so when it is not dangerous at all, or will he avoid putting out his hand to everything because of his mother's shout?

The shout itself is most important in a dangerous situation. The child must not be allowed to burn his hand to learn from the experience. But the mediating value of the shout is very limited. The shout will have value only if it is heard in a proximal time period as the event is occurring and is followed by an explanation that will cause the child to understand why he must avoid reaching for and touching the fire. This should extend beyond the immediate exposure to anything whose temperature is so high that it is liable to cause burning. Thus, when the child withdraws his hand, we have to ask ourselves whether anything remains in this hand of that same instruction that caused the child to withdraw. Did the hand respond only to a message that passed through it, or was information impressed on it that will cause it to be extended or not extended in different situations, in other places, and at other times? There is a potential danger here. One must be careful that the mother's shout not be generalized to other situations that are not dangerous, and that the shout is not projected to any situation of risk, challenge, or novelty that eventually limits the child's behavioral options.

Conveying the mediator's meaning to the recipient of the mediation, whether it be a child or an adult, raises a potential ethical question—what gives another person the right to enforce his or her subjective meaning on other individuals? And indeed, we have observed increasing tendencies in many cultures leading to the reduction of mediated interventions and limiting interactions only to those that satisfy the primary needs and stimuli considered essential for the development of the child. This is seen among parents and educators who question the ethical basis of the mediation of meaning. These tendencies have become a part of many educators' ideology, according to which the transmission of meaning by a mediator with intentions is not desirable, because it is far too close to dogmatism and indoctrination.

Those who follow this ideology ignore the limitations and damage of an interaction that rejects the mediation of meaning. The absence of meaning influences both the mediator or teacher and the student or mediatee, from the standpoint of the amount of the interaction, its nature, and its force—not only between the teacher and the student, but also between it (the organism) and the environment. In interactions that reject the mediation of meaning, emotional components are also missing. A parent or any other mediator who does not impart meaning to his or her children impoverishes their lives not only of contents, values, and motives, but also withholds from them the very propensity and the need to look for, and even to build for, themselves the meaning of their lives and deeds.

Here we come to the second contribution of the mediation of meaning—the generation of the need of the mediatee to look for meanings for oneself. By this we mean not only to search for the specific meaning that the mediator tries to convey, but also the search for associations and connections between events and phenomena—in the broader sense of cause and purpose. The specific meanings mediated to the child by an adult mediator can be forgotten or be modified with time. But the need and the orientation to search for meaningfulness, which is instilled by the mediator, become a permanent existential need. Human beings in whom this orientation is lacking, and who do not look for meaning, are deprived both in the cognitive and emotional sense, and in all the elements that affect the motivational and energetic dimensions of life.

The mediated propensity of the individual to search for and build meanings for one's life is the factor and driving force of the transformations and challenges that will be undergone, because transitions and changes during life require the person to adapt the new situations to the meanings that have been assigned to previous situations in life.

ESTABLISHING THE CONDITIONS FOR MLE: A SUMMARIZATION

Mediation is, therefore, a universal phenomenon, which is not dependent on language, contents, culture, geographical location, or any other variable.

It is that which makes humans capable of adapting to the changes and transitions in our life experience and transmitting our culture from generation to generation. In order for the interaction to possess a mediating value, it must include—in an active consciously provided manner—the qualities of intention and reciprocity, the mediation of transcendence, and the search for (and discovery of) meaning in the functioning of the mediatee and others.

Mediated learning experience—as an interaction with a unique quality—is what creates human beings' flexibility, sensitivity, readiness, and desire to understand what is going on, and capacity to generalize it over and above the isolated phenomenon that is being experienced. The mediation of transcendence is responsible for the constant expansion of the human need system beyond the primary, biological needs and the emergence of special spiritual, moral, and aesthetic needs. Of all the characteristics of mediated learning experience, the mediation of meaning is that which is determined (and contributes) to the greatest extent by our cultural heritage. Meaningfulness reflects values, customs, and norms that regulate and shape shared and inherited behaviors. However, over and above any cultural experience, the mediated quality of meaning is expressed by a change that it brings about in learning—by rendering it understood, strengthened, integrated, and, in the final analysis, internalized as a system of principles whose guiding force is over and above the specific content in which it was acquired.

CHAPTER 7

Mediating for Human Diversity: Building Positive Attitudes Toward Learning

In the previous chapter we described the universal parameters that are essential to the existence of an interaction with a mediating quality. These parameters are responsible for the necessary flexibility, plasticity, and modifiability common to all people wherever they are.

There are, however, other important parameters of mediated learning experience (MLE) that contribute to the diversity of human learning and development. In this chapter we shall describe them. They are the dimensions of MLE that reflect the development of the unique reactions and potentials for modifiability for every human being and every culture. These parameters of MLE derive from specific situations in the particular cultures that the mediator and the mediatee belong to. They are a reflection of the given ecology of the culture and the unique characteristics of each and every human being that are responsible for the sometimes vast differences in the quality of parent–child interactions in the same family, and even between parents and their identical twins.

We have identified nine parameters that—in contrast to the three essential characteristics that we discussed in the previous chapter—have the potential to enrich the character of the MLE. To reiterate their importance, these parameters are responsible for the emergence of the diversification between cultures and between human beings. We cannot explain the origin of this diversification other than by pointing to the mediating processes responsible for the transmission of values, styles, areas of interest, and forms of behavior.

These parameters were chosen from two points of view: the first is a consideration of the particular needs of our age, which demand constant adaptation to the technological and cultural changes imposed on us; and the second is a focus on those individuals who, for a variety of reasons, have not had sufficient access to MLE.

We will now offer brief descriptions of each of these parameters.

MEDIATION OF FEELINGS OF COMPETENCE

For human beings to act with confidence, meet challenges, and cope with situations that are new for them, they must feel that they are competent to control these situations—to overcome difficulties, become familiar with the new and the unknown, and approach them with the expectation they will master them.

We must distinguish between the feeling of competence and competence itself. Individuals can be competent and capable without feeling that they are indeed such. Many people function at a low level because they lack a *sense* of competence, at times in contrast to their true ability. Great artists occasionally report a sense of being an impostor or of representing themselves as being more than they really are. This feeling is an expression of a lack of a sense of competence, self-worth, and personal esteem. Such individuals feel, unjustifiably, that they are deceiving their audience, as if what they are showing is not really within their grasp.

The feeling of competence does not come into existence in human beings on its own, and it is not an unavoidable product of the conditions of human existence. Developing a feeling of competence requires experiencing feedback. For example, consider a human mediator who interprets the mediatee's behavior as testifying to control and ability and brings this to the awareness of the mediatee, creating not only competence to do things, but also—and most importantly—the feeling of competence to perform them.

To create in the mediatee the feeling of ability, the mediator assigns tasks that are situated at a certain distance from immediate reach and therefore require effort. The mediator provides the mediatee with tools for coping with the new tasks and explains the resulting successful functioning (with the help of mediation) as an expression of competence.

This function of the mediator, even though it appears simple, is not for many mediators. Let us observe, for example, the behavior of a mother who is swimming with her little daughter in a swimming pool:

> The mother, a faster swimmer than her daughter, says to her: "You see, I have finished first!" She repeats this a few times. The girl tries to fight against the injustice of the contest and says: "But I was tired . . . but you are much longer than me." Her complaints are rejected by the mother, who again repeats: "But I finished before you."

The mother tried to get the girl to succeed by pushing her to greater achievements than those she was capable of achieving at her age. However, the girl did not derive a feeling of competence from this experience, and it is doubtful if the girl, in this encounter, will consider herself as a person with ability—even if she does experience higher achievements in the future.

This attitude is unfortunately also widespread in schools. In many contemporary schools, across a wide diversity of cultures, it is considered that the best way to get children to achieve is to evaluate only their products and to give them proficiency marks for them. This approach often has a negative impact on the feeling of ability, even when it increases the immediate achievements. In such situations, many children turn into underachievers in the wake of generalized and unjust feedback of this kind. If the marks do not reflect either the students' immediate level of functioning or the level of improvement that they achieved in relation to their initial performance, they will offer no sense of accomplishment other than a general comparison to their peers, which can exaggerate feelings of incompetence. Subsequently, students' readiness to invest effort to make progress deteriorates, and in the end they are liable to see themselves as failures in spite of objectively positive performance. It is not hard to see this as leading to such long-term consequences as affective disengagement and dropping out of school.

To create in learners a feeling of ability and competence, the mediator must initiate mediated interactions that are aimed at imparting feelings of ability and competence. To this end, one must offer the learner interpretations of the successful experience they have undergone, which makes them aware of the significance of their success and the connection between the proof of their ability in one task and further successes in many other tasks.

The feeling of ability and competence is likely to play a crucial role in the individual's adaptation to new situations because one must feel a general sense of ability in order to have the courage necessary to take on challenges, to investigate realities, and to perform unfamiliar and novel tasks. The conditions of human survival are not necessarily the source of a feeling of competence. The feeling of competence is the outcome of the mediation that a person gains from a mediator who interprets various responses as an expression of will and ability. In general, then, the feeling of competence derives from the readiness of the environment (interpreted by MLE) to clearly convey the person's actions and successes as an expression of abilities that often go beyond subjective feelings and evaluations of their value (to self and others).

MEDIATION OF REGULATION AND CONTROL OF BEHAVIOR

The regulation of behavior is turned in two directions. The first direction is toward the restraining of responses. When I encounter a stimulus of any kind, I am inclined to respond immediately, but I restrain myself, giving myself time to think, to check whether I possess all the data required for responding adequately, and, if I lack data, to look for and have all of the required data before I react. The regulation of behavior should be, therefore, a voluntary act, the outcome of the decision to suspend my response until I have checked out the situation to which I am exposed. But regulation of behavior also has a second, contrasting direction—there are situations that demand an accelerated response, a quick action. Sometimes rapid action may be required in emergency situations or situations requiring immediate response. In these conditions, regulation of behavior takes a different tack, encouraging rapid and timely reactions in order to help those who are immobilized—who are "struck dumb," who freeze in their tracks—to react.

The regulation of behavior is thus a product of an individual's ability to impose thinking on actions—to examine oneself, to assess the situation, and to decide how and when to react. To regulate the behavior of the mediatee, mediators have to act in two stages: in the first stage, they impart to the mediatee the ability to employ the cognitive functions that will enable the performance of the actions required to make a decision about the manner of responding.

In the second stage, the mediator has to calibrate the insight that the mediatee has gained in relation to the planning process based on an assessment of the situation. The mediator has to consider the data and their significance, decide whether to carry out the specific response that was planned, and, if the response is carried out, to impart the ability to decide how, where, when, and in what way to implement it.

This parameter is close to the concept of metacognition as it is used in cognitive psychology. These thinking processes are frequently met with impatience by teachers who view the pupil as a product. In such situations, teachers may interpret the delaying of the response as evidence of a lack of command of the study material. Here, the mediation of regulation and control of behavior requires the mediatee to consider the potential behaviors and responses—to think about them, analyze them, and ultimately generalize from them.

The mediation of regulation of behavior, in the sense of restraining impulsiveness and delaying the action, is not significant to the same extent in every culture. There are cultures that do not encourage the postponement of gratification and the planning of behavior. In these cultures, impulsive and uncontrolled responses to certain stimuli (like situations of tragedy, failure, and bad behavior) are even encouraged. The complexity of our life, and the conditions in which we are called upon to react, make the ability to regulate behavior in socially and culturally appropriate ways critical for us. Therefore, mediators in all the educational frameworks must mediate to the person not only the ability but also the orientation and the awareness of the need to regulate behavior.

MEDIATION OF SHARING BEHAVIOR

In our world—a world in which there are many situations of social alienation, where individualism is increasingly valued, and is, at times, extreme, the ability to share experiences with our fellow human beings and to participate in their experiences is most necessary and desirable.

In the big cities, hundreds of people can live in the same building in the closest of physical proximity and not know one another or greet one another when they meet by chance. Thus, a primary (and some would say existential) need of human beings to share experiences with their fellow man is continually decreasing. Perhaps it is safer and more immediately comfortable to reduce or avoid potential areas of friction. But for many, the consequence is a sense of isolation and even social alienation.

The mediated interaction of sharing behavior is designed to restore to us the readiness and ability to make contact and arrive at a meeting with our fellow human beings, and to increase in us the ability to rub shoulders with one another, to adjust ourselves to one another, to gain insight and support from one another, and to create a harmony between our experiences with one another.

There are cultures in which cognitive, emotional, and even ritual participation with our fellows represents a central need for a person. I still recall the embarrassment I felt years ago when I was given the unpleasant task of reporting a young girl's inappropriate behavior to her parents:

> The mother wept aloud and invited all the neighbors to come and hear how miserable she was. The news spread rapidly, women and children entered crying and mourning, while the mother repeated the description of the shame and pain that the daughter had visited on the family. Instead of hiding her shame, the mother turned it into public knowledge.
>
> In similar fashion, many children made public in the boarding school the extremely unpleasant news that had reached them in letters they had received from home, as if the only way for them to experience the reality of the letter was to increase its significance by sharing it with others.

Other cultures attach importance to secrecy and the right of a person to absolute privacy. Sometimes the need for privacy attains such proportions that a person is not supposed to appear before another person while eating a meal. But despite the intercultural differences, some aspect of interpersonal sharing of experience is a universal phenomena and is experienced at very early stages of life. Young children tend to point to everything that they see, as if seeking (and needing) to share with others the experience they have undergone. At later stages, other manifestations of emotion, such as crying or laughter, constitute a way for the "I" to impose itself on the other in a potential effort to cause someone outside the self to participate in an emotional experience.

In our day, the need and readiness to share with others our experiences and to participate in their experiences is an adaptational necessity. In the social conditions in which a person is liable to find oneself, the educational value of the mediation of sharing is not confined to the emotional aspect, but there is in it the potential to enrich a person's treasury of mental-cognitive behaviors. One of the outstanding examples of this is the autistic person whose spiritual poverty derives from being unable to share with one's fellow human beings and to participate with them in shared experiences.

The mediation of sharing behavior also goes in two directions. The recipient of my sharing participates in that which is significant to me, confirming my experience, and I hear myself conveying my experience to others, further reinforcing the meaning and integrity of my experience.

MEDIATION OF INDIVIDUALIZATION
AND PSYCHOLOGICAL DIFFERENTIATION

Parallel to, and perhaps in contrast to, the mediation of sharing, it is no less important to build into a human being a feeling of individualization, of being a separate entity, with the right to think and to express oneself in a special way that is distinct from that of others. What appears on initial reflection to be paradoxical—sharing as against individualization—is not contradictory, but rather complementary in the human being.

We are individuals, but at the same time we belong to and with others— our parents, our families, our communities, our culture—both as partners and as separate and distinct individuals. Today an adaptive person has to be activated by these two components together—that is to say, you have to be yourself while also being a partner to others. Teachers who know how to mediate these two components enable pupils to express themselves and their positions and do not impose one or the other aspect of experience on the pupil.

But unfortunately this often does not occur. In general, learners are compelled to make their style and attitudes correspond to that which is acceptable to the teacher. More and more, in many cultures, a lack of individualization has become the norm.

The need for individualization and psychological differentiation is not observed in equal measure in every culture or every family. It is influenced more than any other component by the demands of society. For example, big differences can be found among cultures in relation to terms of dependence and independence among males and females arising from the different roles that each society assigns to gender. In Western culture, the need for individualization and psychological differentiation is particularly stressed. But it may derive from the absence of mediational interaction that pushes children into a premature independence situation, more than from an action directed and supported by a mediator.

Individualization and psychological differentiation can be developed through a process of mediation that is preceded and accompanied by mediation of sharing behavior and emotional involvement along with mediation of meaning and of transcendence and intentionality and reciprocity, which are the basis of the mediated interaction (what we refer to in the preceding chapter as the core conditions for MLE). In this way, feelings of rejection and abandonment can be avoided—children whose confidence level is fortified through a process of mediation display a far better ability to perceive themselves as separate and independent entities, possessing emotional ties that continue way beyond the separation that is anchored in space and time.

On the other hand, children who have not been fortified by means of a mediational interaction react in panic to separations from their parents, home, and other familiar attachments because it is difficult for them to imagine themselves as living without the physical presence of these attachments.

The mediatee's awareness of the legitimacy of differences of opinions, tendencies, desires, and styles, without necessarily accepting them, represents an important condition for a proper individuation process. Mediation that looks for and values the differences between individuals and their unique behaviors leads to the formation of a distinct and acceptant self-perception in relation to others.

On the other hand, if individuation is created through enforced physical separation without the prerequisite mediation which we described earlier in this chapter, it will not lead to true psychological differentiation. In many cases it constitutes the basis for the development of an extremely egoistic and egocentric personality that does not identify its boundaries and thus does not perceive itself as a distinct and independent entity.

A good developmental example is the infant, who in its first days does not differentiate between itself and the mother. The moment it begins to recognize the separateness between them (in a process of individuation and differentiation) there begins a process of connection and a potential for estrangement that is, in fact, a sign of its developmental process as a human entity. As the philosopher Martin Buber says, in order for there to be relations there has to be distance. Therefore, the greater the (potential) distance, so the deeper the relationship can become.

MEDIATION OF GOAL SEEKING, GOAL SETTING, AND GOAL ACHIEVING

The presence of a goal in the individual's mental repertoire reflects the beginning of a representational (abstract) modality of thinking. The mediator presents to the mediatee a range of potential goals, many of which enlarge the mediatee's sphere of awareness as to what is possible, desirable, and attainable. The achievement of goals presents a prospect of the future, growing increasingly distant, demanding the rejection of more immediate gratifications, and creates tension between the volition—the need—and the meeting of it.

Meeting the need is set as a goal distant in time and place. The possibility of living and experiencing not in what exists but in what is desirable—in the potential, in the anticipated—and the ability to set goals that are situated in the distance is what causes the human being to use abstract forms of thinking—the imagination—in the representation of what is not yet in existence.

In setting ourselves goals as mediators, and in gradually distancing them from the mediatee, we contribute to the diminution of the needs and impulses that demand immediate satisfaction. Subsequently, this process has an extremely important role in the structuring of higher mental operations, which characterize human intelligence. The ability to select goals, to prefer certain goals over others, and to acquire the means for achieving those goals are all abilities that the mediator creates in the mediatee, and thereby enables the attainment of higher levels of functioning.

Setting distant goals and investing in plans and actions in order to achieve them, in spite of the fact that they will be achieved only in the future, is what creates a transcendental value—the broadening of the mental field and a sense of expanded time and space. Perhaps this is one reason why the literary genre of science fiction is so popular and compelling.

An example of this can be found in the parable of the very old man who plants a carob tree. A passerby asks him, "Why are you planting that tree? You surely know that you will not manage to eat its fruits because that tree will only produce fruit in another seventy years." The old man answers, "Yes, I know, but if my parents had not done what I am doing today I would not have been able to eat carobs."

MEDIATION OF THE SEARCH FOR
CHALLENGE, NOVELTY, AND COMPLEXITY

Meeting a challenge means being ready to be involved not only in a familiar area that we are used to engaging in but also in newer and more complex areas of activity. There are cultures that are careful to remove such challenges from the young person, perhaps to insulate the child from frustration, discomfort, or failure. But in the modern world, with the rapid and sharp changes that are an inseparable part of it, a person will be unable to adapt unless he or she can meet the challenges of the novel and unfamiliar.

A challenge is, in its essence, distant from us. We mentioned the element of distance in connection with the mediation of transcendence and the achievement of goals, and we need to refer to it again. Meeting a challenge is accompanied by distancing, for we relate to something that does not exist by engaging now in order to achieve potential outcomes in the future, which may not be immediately anticipated.

The mediation of challenging behavior must represent a goal in all the programs that seek to increase the adaptability of the individual to the changes and complexities of our world. Today's individual is required to cope with complex tasks, the like of which have never before been experienced. Answers such as "I didn't hear," "I didn't learn," or "I have never performed such a task" are dysfunctional in situations of constant change. The readiness to learn and move from known situations to the unknown as well as the tendency to confront challenging novelty and complexity and not to give up are essential for our adaptation. The MLE interaction plays an important role in this realization.

The most effective way to foster a readiness to respond positively to challenging situations is to encourage parents and other caregivers to avoid overprotecting the individual in nondangerous situations. Differences observed in the reactions of individuals to new food, new clothes, and new demands present challenges from the familiar but can be mediated to great effect to encourage curiosity, acceptance, and the eventual broadening of the learner's repertoire of experience. One of the significant differences existing between cultures is manifested by the way in which the individual is required to meet challenges. We have observed children who seldom have been mediated for the acceptance and mastery of challenge become literally immobilized when, as older individuals, they must respond to new or changing demands.

MEDIATION OF THE AWARENESS
OF BEING A MODIFIABLE ENTITY

In addition to the biological changes and the growth associated with age, human beings must perceive themselves, and be perceived by others, as possessing a continuous identity. But does this mean that they must also see themselves as being unmodifiable, with innate and unchangeable character traits? To the extent that this is experienced or expected (implicitly or explicitly), there is a danger that a kind of pessimism will pervade the educational systems to which people are exposed, and in relation to the situation of people in general—in all areas of their lives. This pessimistic approach clearly derives from a deterministic outlook, according to which the probability of change is extremely low. It leads to a sharp differentiation in everything to do with setting goals and choosing the means to achieve them in education, employment, rehabilitation, and even in the penal system. From this deterministic point of view, whoever can show signs of correct development doesn't need any investment of effort, and whoever shows signs of inadequate development would not benefit from investment of effort.

The notion that a human being is modifiable, without connection to the developments determined by biological factors, is not particularly accepted (even in cultures that hold themselves to be open and individualistic). Quite frequently, we hear parents and teachers say: "What can one expect from him? You know how he is. He doesn't change; he won't change. One can predict what he will do, how he will behave, and what he will achieve."

Such an approach is liable to have two disastrous outcomes. Those who function well may possibly not do enough or may not do anything to maintain their performance level or even to improve it. Perhaps this explains why gifted children are sometimes underachieving. On the other hand, why should low-functioning people invest effort to improve their situation if they (or those around them) are convinced that their situation is unmodifiable?

The assumption regarding the existence of these innate traits stands in the way and paradoxically blocks the possibility of modifiability—a possibility that is crucial for adaptation. The person says: "How will I be able to do this? I am like this. That is how everyone knows me, and that is how I shall be." And if one dares to think of the possibility of modifying oneself, someone will take care to remind him or her (directly or by implication): "Hey, don't you forget who you are. After all, we know you!"

The mediator must therefore work actively to create in the person the feeling of his or her being modifiable. Parents who point out to their children how they have changed for the better as a result of taking certain actions create in their children an awareness of the possibility and necessity of making an effort to achieve their goals of development and improvement. Mediation of modifiability, as a uniquely human characteristic, is critical for increasing the potential of the mediatee to adapt through the experience of an autoplasticity, a welcome addition (but not a substitute) to the preservation of identity.

The belief in the ability of individuals to increase their modifiability will bring educators to search for signs of change when evaluating the individual and to give a more dynamic (and optimistic) prognosis that takes into account the changes that have occurred, rather than solely basing evaluation on the existing level of functioning. Consider the ultimate optimism of using this approach as a prediction of future functioning.

The procedures and instruments that we developed in order to assess (as opposed to test) the modifiability of the examinee, which we call the Learning Propensity Assessment Device (LPAD), is based on this belief. Chapter 10 is devoted to the LPAD.

MEDIATION OF OPTIMISTIC ALTERNATIVES

When faced by different possibilities for action or choice, some people will tend to select the pessimistic alternative. Unfortunately, this can be a self-fulfilling prophesy.

The posture of pessimism occasionally has a magic goal. In order not to "give the Devil a chance to harm us!" or conversely to defend ourselves from disappointment we prepare ourselves for the worst outcomes, thereby being in a kind of control. The choice of a pessimistic alternative induces passivity in the one who chooses it: "I don't have any chance of this, so it's not worthwhile for me to invest effort or even to make the effort." On the other hand, the choice of an optimistic alternative—the knowing that it is possible—creates in a person an impulse to mobilize the means and the forces required to realize it. It also imposes a responsibility to act in order to materialize that which we view as possible.

We begin to mediate to children the search for an optimistic alternative at early stages of development when we bring them to expect positive outcomes: "It will be fun," "it will taste good," and so on. The search for an optimistic alternative, and the conveyance of the expectation, leads us to look for and accept change and increases our readiness to attack environmental factors that threaten our physical and mental equilibrium. In this way, we enable the development of the cognitive strategies that become the mental operations of the situations encountered and transcend to future solutions that will be experienced.

MEDIATION OF A SENSE OF BELONGING

The importance of mediation of a sense of belonging varies from culture to culture. Modern Western societies lay stress on the rights of the individual and limit one's readiness to give them up in return for belonging to a broader entity. More traditional societies tend to give preference to the sense of belonging and prepare individuals to surrender a large part of their freedom and the expression of their individualism in exchange for belonging to a reference group.

The phenomenon of alienation, which we can discern over recent decades in Western or "westernized" societies, is closely connected to the isolation of the nuclear family from the wider social units to which it is expected (implicitly) to belong. From this isolation there derive cognitive defects, together with many emotional and social defects. Belonging to the nuclear family alone, without connection to a broader extended family, often creates a lack of connection with the very meaningful intergenerational aspects of our lives. This lack of verticality in the family experience thus creates a lack of continuity beyond time and place. Hence, there develops a feeling of alienation from family, self, and community.

The mediation of a sense of belonging is particularly important during periods in which the isolated nuclear family offers very limited security from the standpoint of its stability as a framework. Consider the incidence of divorce, abandonment, physical isolation, single-parent families, and a whole host of similar conditions that are increasingly experienced across diverse cultures.

In the previous three chapters, we described the mediated learning experience (MLE) as an interaction possessing a special quality, unique to human beings. The mediational interaction between a human being and the world is not random, but derives from the intention of the mediator and his or her desire to transfer it to the mediatee. This is no less true for the sense of belonging, and it is intimately related to the MLE parameters that precede and support it—the transcendence of immediate experience, the achieving of meaningful goals, the sharing of human experiences, and so on.

THE IMPORTANCE OF THE "SITUATIONAL" PARAMETERS OF MLE

These are the factors that create in individuals the conditions required for them to derive benefit from varied learning possibilities, however random and fortuitous they may be. There are three characteristics of MLE that are universal and found in every culture—in every place where human beings take care to transfer their messages to the next generation. These are *intentionality/reciprocity, transcendence,* and *the mediation of meaning.* We reiterate that MLE cannot be effective without these characteristics forming the foundation of the learning experience.

In the current chapter, we have focused on additional characteristics of the mediational interaction. These characteristics create the differences between people and between cultures. There are marked differences between cultures in the degree of importance that they assign to a given experience or encounter, and this can serve as an opportunity to provide MLE. However, the mediator must be alert and ready to exploit those situations when appropriate. To miss them is to miss important opportunities.

THE DIFFERENCES BETWEEN MLE AND PARENTING AND TEACHING

We want to address one more question that arises with some frequency because the answer to it constitutes a good way to sum up the characteristics of a mediated learning experience: What is the difference between the interaction of MLE and "regular" teaching? Are not teachers or parents mediators by definition of their roles?

In answering this question, we shall examine the differences between the two forms of interaction—the mediational role and the "teaching/parenting" interaction. Although in practice we can find common elements in these two roles, they are clearly different.

- The mediator stations him- or herself between the stimulus (S) and the response (R) in such a way that the learner is given the necessary tools to cope with the stimulus and is able to interact with the stimulus gradually (for example, by incrementally raising the level of difficulty of the task or regulating the quantity of data presented to the learner). In contrast to this posture (and intentionality), the teacher or parent frequently stations him- or herself in the learner's place and answers in his stead in order to demonstrate how the learner should cope with the stimulus or the situation presented.

- The mediational interaction is designed to increase the mediatee's learning ability and the modifiability. The teaching or parenting role, on the other hand, aims at transmitting as many skills and as much knowledge and information as possible, usually in response to specific content areas or tasks to be completed.

- The criterion for the success of the mediational interaction experience is the modifiability of the learner and his or her ability to be an independent learner. The regular teaching or parenting interaction measures its success by means of the learner's level of achievement in tests or mastery of specific tasks that indicate the extent to which the learner has absorbed the instruction.

- In the interaction between the three partners of the MLE (the teacher or parent, the learner, and what is to be learned) there are different characteristics in each of the approaches, with a mutual transformation that occurs (see a discussion of these transformations in an earlier section of this book). In the mediational interaction, the mediator brings the learner to the task, directs activity toward the solution, creates conditions that allow the learner to arrive independently at the correct answer, encourages successes, and reinforces feelings of competence. The mediator prevents the learner from making mistakes and builds learning situations that are intended for success. The mediator expends considerable efforts in developing the learning and thinking processes of the learner as well as an awareness of the processes occurring. In contrast, the teacher or parent focuses on bringing the material to the learner, correcting incorrect responses, covering as much material as possible, and producing correct answers or positive responses, and does not necessarily (or overtly) focus on the processes (strategies) used to arrive at them.

We accept that trained and effective teachers, like active and concerned parents, will engage in many mediational interactions and integrate them into the teaching process, but they might not do so in a systemic and intentional manner. Moreover, in situations of educational or parental necessity, the frameworks in which their characteristic roles and activities are conducted are far from being ideal for activating MLE objectives. In Chapter 13 we shall deal with the environmental characteristics that enable mediation or block it.

At the same time, we acknowledge that there are necessary direct interactions with the world and a need for simple and direct means of transmitting information. These do and must exist as a parallel system to MLE. The critical aspect is to know when, where, how, and to what extent to activate and nurture the differences.

CHAPTER 8

The Nature of Learning in the Absence of Mediated Learning Experience

The mediational interaction possesses special qualities, as we have described in earlier chapters, but the learner cannot make contact with the world only by means of mediation. In life, most of the interactions between the person and the environment take place directly, without mediation. The mediator is positioned between the person and the world that knocks on the gates of the learner's senses, and yet he or she spontaneously mediates only a small part of the potential interactions for brief periods of time.

However, even in these limited interactions, the mediator creates in the learner the tools required to derive benefit from the direct exposure to stimuli. Thus, we are talking about the existence of two parallel modalities of interaction: the direct, which takes place most of the time, and the mediated, which possesses the power to create in a person the necessary components for modification.

The MLE interaction is capable, therefore, of influencing the quality of a person's direct interaction with the world, and its absence is liable to result in the learner's inability to derive crucial benefits from the plethora of direct exposure experiences. Consequently, we come across many people who are not capable of deriving benefit from their direct encounter with the world and with the stimuli around them. The absence of exposure to MLE makes it very difficult for them to derive benefit even from their own experiences.

WHAT CAUSES THE ABSENCE OF MLE?

Two groups of factors are generally responsible for the absence of MLE: One group is that of environmental factors and manifests itself in the absence of mediators. The second group is that of the internal barriers that exist in a student, which do not allow the reception of the mediation that is offered. This second group of barriers is connected to the biological, psychological, physical, and mental components of the person that make him or her inaccessible to mediation.

In certain environments there is a sort of chain of causes for the absence of mediation: for example, among people who live in situations of physical poverty. In such situations, the constant concern of parents for their very subsistence may prevent them from mediating to their children and transmitting to them their culture—the ways of thinking that have developed in them as a result of intergenerational cultural mediation. So the chain of mediation is severed, and there is created an absence of mediation. The chain is broken when parents who have experienced the mediation of their culture do not transmit it to their children. They do not mediate between their children and the world—namely, they do not interpret, label, identify, and ascribe significance to the phenomena their children encounter. Thus, a child who is not mediated passes through the world without deriving benefit from contact with it and becomes an adult who has not been mediated and may not mediate to his or her children.

The culture of poverty often creates a situation where preference is given to the ability of the individual to survive in the short term over the quality of life or long-term survival. If I have to care for my children so they do not die of hunger, I do not worry whether they eat before or after they wash (or if they wash at all) or if they eat on the floor or on a white tablecloth. In a culture of poverty the first priority is given to an interaction that enables survival. The mediation of the transmission of values, experience, and cultural treasures of the past is pushed aside and may never be addressed.

At the same time, there are cultures in which poor parents are prepared to go without food for their children to receive cultural transmission. There have been wonderful examples of this phenomenon in villages in Poland—mothers would give up their crust of bread for their children to be able to attend classes. That is to say, when there exists a culture of mediation, of cultural transmission from generation to generation, the priorities change even in a situation of harsh struggles for survival.

MEDIATING THE PAST AND THE FUTURE

The absence of cultural mediation exists not only in poor societies; there are societies who stop mediating their past to the next generations and thus put an end to their existence as separate and unique cultures. But not to mediate the past also means not to mediate the future, because the future is a function of the past. The absence of mediation affects not only the knowledge of the child, but also those dimensions of existence that are not possible for a person unless he or she relates to the past. The philosopher Henry Bergeson put the connection between the past and the future very well when he compared it to the process of shooting an arrow: The tauter the bowstring is pulled, the further the arrow's flight.

Here we wish to bring up a question that you may possibly have asked yourselves when considering Bergeson's metaphor: What is the connection between cultural transmission and the firing of arrows? Or, in other words, why is the active and directional mediation of the past and of cultural heritage so important for building the future?

To answer these questions, let us go back for a moment and recall two of the functions of the mediator: conveying knowledge and experience that would not be accessible to the learner but for the mediator providing it and creating in the learner of forms of thinking and cognitive abilities that do not exist except by virtue of the mediation.

With regard to the mediation of the subject matter content, or in the wider sense the mediation of knowledge, we must remember that there is knowledge that the person will never acquire spontaneously and will not be known except through the mediator. The person who takes care to bring content to the mediatee is exercising a quality of intervention that we have defined and described as the MLE parameter of intentionality. For example, everything that exists over the horizon of time and our vision, such as the infiniteness of the world, must be mediated to us. Without mediation we would remain ignorant, always having to "begin from the beginning" and to reactivate all the mechanisms of our thinking. Ultimately, a human being's existence depends on (and wants to acquire) understanding and the collection of information that opens one to the knowledge of the infiniteness of the world. Alternatively, what would the individual know about the past if it were not for someone mediating what happened before the time that was immediately and directly experienced? Mediation thus contributes to a sense of past and future as well as to the present.

The mediation of subject matter is very important in itself because it enriches the knowledge and dimensions of a person's existence. But for those of us who are interested in the development of intelligence, thinking, and the modifiability of student potential for learning, it is less interesting. We are interested in the contribution of the mediator to the development of the person's intelligence, and especially the ability to modify oneself and to adapt to the many situations which one is exposed to and must cope with on a constant basis.

It is well accepted that a person can also acquire a great deal of knowledge without mediators because one comes into the world potentially equipped with skills that enable continuing development and progress during direct exposure to stimuli (S-O-R). However, a person's modifiability and the plasticity that characterizes it are imparted (facilitated, elaborated, and so forth) through the experience of mediation.

Herein lies one of the great differences between our conception and that of Piaget. He makes the development of human intelligence conditional on the maturation of the nervous system. According to Piaget, a person maintains active interaction with the world according to the level of maturity of the organism. We maintain that the Piagetian conception does not allow one to fully explain the existing variations of the development of intelligence and its components—the modifiability of a person and the great difference between people and their level of functioning.

MLE AND CULTURAL TRANSMISSION

We assume that cultural heritage and its collective needs are transmitted to the individual by means of the mediated interaction of transcendence, and thus the culture perpetuates itself without an absolute and direct relation to its contents, the linguistic richness that is manifested in interaction, or the level of awareness of the mediatee to the transmission process itself.

Mediation in this sense—that is to say, the mediation for learning and the acquisition of modifiability—is not connected to specific contents or to specific cultures, irrespective of the extent to which the individual preserves the specific content of the culture. Therefore, the tendency to ascribe the existence of MLE (exclusively or predominantly) to Western culture and not to developing countries (what used to be called the Third World) has no grounding in reality. In developing countries, there are many children who are given marvelous mediation through their families and communities: The Yemenite child and the Moroccan child who have learned in their community- and culture-based schools; the children who have immigrated from Ethiopia to Israel and received intensive mediation in a different environment; the Bedouin families who preserve their culture under extreme conditions of economic and physical stress. The same can be said of African Americans and the many Native American tribes that have preserved their traditions in spite of systematic attempts by the dominant culture to eradicate them. Children who receive mediation in these situations have acquired cognitive structures and forms of learning that enable them to adapt when necessary to a completely different life from that of their culture without abandoning their cultural heritages.

Therefore, it is not the cultural content but the cultural transmission and the quality of the interaction in which it is performed that create the substantial difference in the ability of adaptation between those whose culture was transmitted to them and those whose culture has been held back from them. A person who has undergone a process of learning about a culture, even if it is a very primary culture (one that is usually and unjustifiably termed *primitive*), will have the tools that enable the acquisition of any new culture to which he or she is exposed.

In 1965, Lesser, Fifer, and Clark (1965) conducted a seminal study that examined four immigrant groups in the United States (Chinese, Jewish,

African American, and Hispanic Americans) to determine the degree to which they used their cultural heritage to enable their offspring to adapt to and integrate into the new culture. Parents who systematically transmitted their cultures to their children prepared them to adapt to new and different cultural experiences and gave them the necessary tools to relate to new experiences without losing their cultural heritages. We generalize from findings such as these to point out that children who are deprived of their culture will not have adaptive mechanisms, and those who have been mediated in their culture will have a propensity to learn. Put another way, *cultures do not deprive, but one can be deprived of his or her culture, with damaging effects.* We further suggest that using our definition of cultural deprivation, children will find it difficult to derive benefit from direct experiences and will require intensive experiences of mediated learning in order to complete what they missed through the absence of mediation of their culture. In today's climate of child development and parental interactions, more and more children can be seen as culturally deprived as they are exposed to limited MLE in the parental, family, and even community context.

The phenomenon of being severed from the heritage of the past characterizes the culture of immigrants, especially in a society that does everything to induce immigrants to forget about their previous cultural existence and to ensure a rapid absorption into the new culture. The immigrant tells his child: "You don't need to know what I was; it is of no importance whatsoever. Now you must be what you are in order to live in the 'new society.'"

The concept of the melting pot in the United States conveyed this value, and to some extent it was the value at the beginning of the State of Israel. Social critics have concluded that this attitude caused a good deal of damage to the integration of the immigrants. In the United States, there was an active discouragement of holding on to the original culture—it was believed that one could not be a fully integrated American if one did not abandon his or her roots. Yet, we now know that if individuals learn their own culture, they will better adapt to the new culture without abandoning their original heritage. In recent years, as the importance of the need for cultural transmission has been understood, the "melting pot" has been replaced with the new metaphor of the "tossed salad," wherein subgroups are all in the same bowl but retain their individual identities. In this more insightful posture, there is more recognition and effort in communities today to find ways to preserve more of their past and to transmit their cultures to their children. We may also add that this benefit accrues not only to the children but enriches the lives of the adults as well.

COPING WITH THE NEED TO MEDIATE

A unique phenomenon of coping with the need to mediate can be found among the courtesans, the concubines who were in the princely courts of the monarchies. Those courtesans who had children placed them in monasteries or in foster families, and when their children were brought to visit they would hide their faces in veils to avoid being identified.

The courtesan did not mediate the reality to her children as it was, but as she wished it to be. She changed the miserable reality of her life and transmitted to her children "a desirable reality" precisely out of concern that there be a continuity that she mediated to them. This kind of mediation for continuity is derived from the desire to protect her children and to prevent them from continuing the sequence of her unsavory life.

In contrast to situations where there exists the need to mediate, let us consider others—such as the drug addict or murderer—who do not care how or what their children experience and therefore do not try to change the reality of their lives.

In today's world we observe a very problematic tendency among parents, even in well-functioning family systems: For ideological reasons, many have given up their influence with their children or delegated it to others—teachers, caregivers, even the media. They believe: "What right do we have to impose ourselves on the next generation? We must let our children live their lives; we have no right to mediate to them." These parents do not share themselves with their children, and do not see them as continuing their spiritual existence beyond their biological existence.

This phenomenon is becoming so common as to take on epidemic proportions—a mass phenomenon. Its main message is: "What will happen to my children, beyond their physical existence and their ability to receive what is needed in order to achieve a certain quality of life, is not my concern and is not within my power. I don't consider myself responsible for their spiritual or mental condition."

This is a tremendous change in comparison with the patterns of behavior and values that were prevalent in the past, when people assigned the utmost importance to continuity of ethical, religious, and behavioral points of view, and from the standpoint of the preservation of one's good name and social status. Today we meet parents who have no interest whatsoever in such continuity, do not understand its importance, and do nothing to ensure that their children will propagate their heritage. An example of this phenomenon is the counterculture movement of the 1960s in the United States.

There is also unconscious lack of mediation due to the failure to understand the unique significance of the experience of the mediational interaction. We shall illustrate this by giving an example of an interaction that is apparently mediational between two parents and their child (Feuerstein, R., et al. 1988).

Evelyn, the daughter of a prominent family known for its high cultural standards and its contribution to charity, was lacking in mediational learning. It appears she had a mild genetic defect that was considered to be holding up her development. Therefore, her parents were content to surround her with exciting stimuli but did not mediate them to her.

When we met Evelyn for the first time, we were immediately struck by her childish social behavior, her amazing lack of knowledge, and her even more amazing lack of appropriate cognitive activity. She described how she had been left alone with her toys, the television, the stereo, and the computer without mediation. She remembered her childhood as a collection of pictures without anyone to help her to connect them and to assign them any significance.

Evelyn received intensive experience in mediated learning that included our Instrumental Enrichment program, and after it her functioning was well in line with an average level of intelligence.

It is worth noting here an additional phenomenon of an absence of mediation that derives from emotional disturbances of parents who are not capable of mediating and of not being responsible for the future of their children. This was not the case in Evelyn's experience, but it can occur in other situations.

INTERNAL BARRIERS CAUSING THE ABSENCE OF MEDIATION

We now proceed to the second group of barriers that prevent human beings from receiving or benefiting from mediation. Let us first point out that human beings' development depends on two types of factors, as shown in Figure 8.1:

Figure 8.1. Distal and Proximal Factors of Differential Cognitive Development

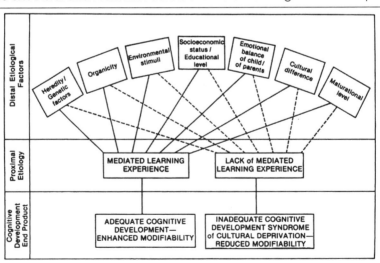

- *Distal factors* (distant, indirect)—those that influence development but do not directly or inevitably influence anticipated outcomes.
- *Proximal factors* (close, direct)—those that determine directly the anticipated and desired outcomes.

Why are there people whose learning ability and whose modifiability is in some way impaired? Many distal causes of their condition can be adduced—problems of the central nervous system, emotional problems, lack of mental maturation, behavioral problems, and so on. The distal factors often determine the intensity of the appearance of the proximal factor, in our formulation the provision of MLE. That is, their presence discourages or may prevent the potential mediator from offering, engaging, or persisting in the provision of MLE and thus lead to the absence of mediation, which becomes the proximal cause for the inability of these people to learn and derive benefit from learning experiences.

The internal barrier can be genetic, chromosomal, the outcome of a prenatal event, or one that occurred during or after birth. The barriers manifest themselves in the difficulty of the child to relate to what the mediator is trying to impart. Barriers of this type are considered in many cases to be impassable. For example, for years it was thought that individuals with Down syndrome had to be accepted as they were. It was assumed that the syndrome, which is expressed in characteristics such as a general hypotonicity, general motoric awkwardness, and an inability to process data created irreversible barriers. Indeed, in such cases, regular mediation is really not useful and will not surmount such barriers. The person with Down syndrome requires a special quality of mediation, numerous repetitions, and a greater intensity of stimulation. One must proceed stage by stage and consider the slow rhythm of development in order to create a learning ability and enable the benefits from direct exposure to stimuli. To elaborate this point, we often recommend that the Down syndrome child not enter kindergarten until the age of 8, giving him or her an opportunity to mature in a more protected environment.

Down syndrome is not the only barrier that requires special mediation. For example, the stimulation threshold of a hyperactive child is different from the stimulation threshold of a hypoactive child, and each of them requires specially adapted MLE. Thus, in order to surmount the internal barriers, it is necessary to tune the mediation in such a way that it will overcome them. If the mediation does not reach the child, MLE does not take place. The mediation is, as we have said, an interaction that takes place only when the loop that is connecting the three participants in the process—the mediator, the stimulus, and the mediatee—is closed (see Figure 6.1 in Chapter 6, and the related discussion of this concept). So long as the mediational loop remains unclosed, the MLE will not take place. To ensure the loop will be closed in such cases, it is necessary to use certain specifically planned and provided elements to overcome the obstacle and to render it passable.

For example, if we succeed in matching the intensities of the stimulus to the type of barrier, a substantial change occurs: those who are considered as lacking the ability to learn—who are, for example, incapable of speech, reading, identifying things, or using their minds—gradually acquire these abilities and become capable beings. We have demonstrated this through the unique methods that we developed with Down syndrome children, children with chromosomal disorders such as Fragile X (broken X chromosome), and other types of disorders that in the past were regarded as unmodifiable.

BREAKING THROUGH THE BARRIERS BY MEANS OF MEDIATION

Every barrier can be crossed if the mediation, as a direct proximal factor, is compatible with the difficulties observed and assessed and reaches the person. We have treated children who, from the standpoint of their thinking capacity, were apparently extremely limited due to a lack of mediation for various reasons. For some the environment did not supply mediation, while internal barriers prevented others from receiving mediation. Consider the conditions of hyperactive or autistic children who are not able to communicate with their environment because of emotional barriers and usually are not affected by normal levels of exposure to mediation.

For children such as these, we created a mediation system that was administered to them by their parents (at least to begin with, because sometimes the parents can do very little for the child who does not accept them. Sometimes, such children cannot be mediated by their parents but are capable of responding to other mediators). As soon as we succeeded in creating an awareness of the proper need for intensity, consistency, and suitable forms of mediation, we succeeded in penetrating the barriers and creating in the children foundations that would enable them to use every exposure to events and experiences to learn. Mediation is liable to modify individuals even when they do not receive it in time and when its absence caused a lack of functioning, and also at later stages in one's life, whether the barriers were generated by environmental sources or from internal sources in the person.

HUMAN BEINGS ARE MODIFIABLE

Thus far, our discussion has pointed out that—despite the factors that have brought individuals to their low levels of functioning and their age or the severity of the condition—if MLE is provided with the quality, intensity, focus, and an understanding of the skills and experiences that need to occur, mediation will have such power that it will penetrate the barriers that existed or that were created due to a lack of mediation. This is the optimistic message of cognitive modifiability and mediated learning experience. With this premise in mind, we can turn to the applications of MLE to exploit the ability of the mind/brain to change and be modified.

CHAPTER 9

Recognizing and Improving Deficient Cognitive Functions

In the previous chapter we described the causes of the absence of mediated learning experience (MLE), and we indicated that they derive from two sources: from an unmediated environment for various reasons (exogenic or environmental factors) and from the internal obstacles preventing human beings from receiving the mediation available and offered (endogenic factors).

The absence of mediation adversely affects not only the human ability to adapt to the necessary and desired changes in the environment and experience but also the thinking and learning processes themselves. We are able to describe the psychological-mental foundations of the thinking, learning, and modification processes that are required for mediation. One such description is a list of cognitive functions that may be deficient or impaired, divided according to the three stages of the mental act: the input phase (the gathering of information), the elaboration phase (the processing of gathered information), and the output phase (the communicating of the outcomes of the two preceding phases). We shall begin by briefly describing the two phases that can be considered peripheral—the input and output—and then discuss what we consider to be the central phase of human mental activity: the elaboration, or process, phase.

When we denote them as deficient functions we are not being negative or pessimistic. Quite the contrary—we identify them as deficient in order to direct our efforts to improving the functions. This expresses an essential optimism: that they can be changed and that we can direct interventions to their modifiability.

THE INPUT PHASE

In this initial phase of mental activity, students collect the data required to perform mental acts. For the data collection to be successful, one is required to perceive stimuli clearly, in a focused, systematic, and exact way and have an ability to relate systematically to different sources of information and stimuli that reach them at the same time. The student must also possess verbal-receptive tools that enable the processing of the information that is perceived (that occurs during the elaboration phase) and must be oriented in space and time to preserve consistencies, scan stimuli consistently, and develop a level of precision and accuracy in the process of data focusing and gathering.

Deficient Functions at the Input Phase

Blurred and sweeping perception. The student who has a clear and focused perception is capable of relating to all the data in his or her possession, to devote the time that is required to each of the components of the phenomenon or the object in a differential manner, and to distinguish between what is important or insignificant, relevant or irrelevant to the task that has to be performed.

With a student or any person who has not received mediation, perception is unclear and all-encompassing instead of being clear and focused. A person with an unclear perception does not pay distinct and separate attention to every stimulus, but "sweeps" the environment and sees it as if enveloped by a mist. Such an individual is not capable of pinpointing from among the data the characteristics that give them significance.

For example, when we show a student with unclear perception the shape of a rectangle and ask for a description of the details of its composition, these details are not perceived, but not because they are not seen. One's vision may be excellent, but there is no focused attention on the details to activate them. Clear perception is not present, and the person will be unable to identify the shape as a rectangle and to distinguish its components by its characteristics (e.g., four sides, each pair of sides parallel and equal in length, and so forth). These data will be lacking when the student must classify the object, compare it to another object, see to which extent it meets certain criteria, and so forth. An interesting, and not unusual, distortion of perception occurs when students are shown a rectangle that is rotated and oriented to stand on its apex (corner). It is often perceived by certain children as a triangle, because the focus is on the apex, and the angled lines radiating from the corner, which is seen (in a somewhat blurred way) as triangular (see discussion of the conservation of constancies below).

Focused perception develops in the course of a process of mediation. This mediation occurs, as we have already described, in the infant's first days: as one learns to focus one's vision on the face of a permanent object—the mother. The infant attaches his or her gaze on her as much as he or she can and learns every small change in her face. At a certain stage the infant begins to relate to the changes that occur in the mother's face and different events and wonders: "What did I do in order for my mother to laugh?"

"What did I do to cause my mother's face to become gloomy?" Infants learn from focusing on the mother's face to focus their gaze on other objects, as well. Children who have no permanent mother-image to focus on find it hard to absorb data and to ascribe consistent significance to them. Studies were conducted by cognitive psychologists J. McV. Hunt and his colleagues describing the lack of focusing and guiding of perception in children raised in orphanages who were deprived of permanent and stable love objects (namely consistent mothering figures).

Impulsive Perception. Students who are random and not systematic in their response to the stimulus world about them, who respond to the first stimulus that they encounter, who jump from one thing to another, and are not capable of performing a systematic process of reflection are manifesting an impulsive perception. This perception can also manifest itself in the difficulty of relating observed phenomena to a particular time and place. Students or individuals who do not know when and where they observed a particular stimulus do not register it in their minds at the time of the event and at the place of its occurrence. In such situations, one lacks the two most important dimensions to define causality: the capacity to locate a stimulus or an event as a reason for an outcome and relate it in time or space to the outcome. We have described the consequence of this deficient function as the lack of systematic searching.

The Lack of the Need for Precision and Accuracy. The general need to be exact develops during the childhood period, following reciprocal activity between children and the people in their environment. There may be cultural differences in the areas in which the need to be exact is stressed. However, from our point of view, there is no particular cultural imperative to this dimension except for the need to be exact in order to gather systematic and accurate information about the world of experience. Children learn that in order to meet with their friends, for example, they need exact details about the time and place of the meeting. We learn through a variety of early experiences that we must be exact in collecting data when we want to compose a full picture from a collection of details, or to see what is the relation between two concepts that we learned—in what way they are alike and in what way they differ. If we are not exact in collecting the data, we shall find it difficult to process them. In any case, the processing will not have the correct significance—or perhaps any significance at all.

Lack of Verbal Labels. The linguistic system—the verbal signs and substitutes of reality—is what enables us to store, remember, and use the data we have perceived. The lack of it—expressed by limitations in naming objects, events, actions, and relations—also causes a lack of ability to distinguish the differences between them and difficulty in encoding and interpreting symbols. Verbal labels enable us to remember, differentiate, and begin to focus and manipulate that which we know.

Difficulty of Placing Oneself in Space and Time. The origin of a deficiency in this function lies in the absence of stable systems of reference to time (when things occur) and space (where they occur). Such a deficiency limits the development and use of concepts for describing the relationships and organization of objects and events in space and time. The lack of this awareness and the concepts developed from them harms the person's ability to represent experience, the ability to create associations between objects and events from the standpoint of the direction, the order, the sequence, and the proximity between them. The deficiencies of situations in time adversely affect the ability of human beings to plan in advance, to think hypothetically, and to deal with the future by way of representation. Also the ability to conceptualize relations of cause and effect depends on a person's command of the concepts of time and space.

The Lack of Preservation of Constancies. This deficiency is manifested by difficulty in preserving characteristics of size, shape, quantity, direction, and the like at the time when a change occurs in any trait or characteristic of the object. The failure to preserve constancy means that objects and events have a very episodic and inconsistent perception, and data that are gathered will be very inconsistent and inaccurate.

Inability to Relate to Multiple Sources of Information Simultaneously. At the input phase, the learner often must perceive, register, and organize multiple sources of information. In such situations, one piece of information must be held in mind while other variables are being considered, without losing the initial information. In this way, all the dimensions of the required information are considered and prepared for the needs of processing them. It is impossible to create associations between objects—to sort them, arrange them, put them in order, and make comparisons between them—if one is not capable of perceiving two pieces of information at the same time. A person with a defective function like this tends to relate to one source of information of any kind and tends to ignore the rest. It is difficult to identify a number of individual sources of information and to combine them in order to create a complete picture. Additionally, in a different but related modality of interaction, with such a deficiency it is difficult to grasp the existence of viewpoints that are different from one's own.

THE OUTPUT PHASE

In the output phase of the mental act, the student formulates the results of the elaboration of gathered information (e.g., thinking): After I have reflected, absorbed, processed, combined data and separated, sorted, and classified them, deciphered them—I am then ready to encode my experience (the data) and create in my thinking a way to solve the problem. I must then formulate the outcomes of my thinking in a way that the correct product will be transmitted. I must formulate them so that they will be received, understood, and accepted by the recipients of the product.

The act of formulating an output that will be clear both to me and to others is likely to be a condition of the existence of a mediational process. For example, if I give an unclear answer to a question and it is accepted as it is, there will not be demands made upon me to reformulate or modify my responses at the output phase. If, on the other hand, I experience an environment that demands a product that is understood, acceptable, and of a certain structural and pragmatic level, my functioning will be enhanced and I will be energized and engaged in the larger process of learning and social development—experiencing the transcendent level of human potential.

Deficient Functions at the Output Phase

Egocentric Communication. This communication deficiency derives from the form of the individual's attitude to one's fellow human being, as one who does not constitute a separate entity. The individual who communicates in an egocentric manner does not feel the need to detail all the information needed to understand the message, because it is assumed that the other knows all that he/she knows. One says to oneself: "If I think in this way they also must think in this way. Therefore, I do not need to convince or explain my position." When they ask: "Why?" the answer is "That's how it is," without any need to explain the reply. The essence of this deficiency is the lack of awareness on the part of the communicator that what is being communicated is not understood and a lack of the need to facilitate understanding.

One overcomes egocentric communication when one grasps that there is a process of individuation (see a description of this parameter of MLE in Chapter 7) that makes people diverse and separate entities. They may or may not have the information or experience that I have. When I take it for granted that they already know what I know, I will not make the effort to assure that they understand what I am communicating, and therefore my communication will be egocentric. Thus it is necessary to acquire the tools to produce an output that will be understood, not only by us, but also by others. Paradoxically, individuals who may have good reception and processing abilities sometimes may or may not have the need to communicate, and might find it difficult to formulate things so that they will be understood by others.

Trial and Error Responses. The behavior of trial and error at the output stage is sometimes a reflection of unplanned data collection at the input stage. One who responds in this way does not learn from experience and is not capable of avoiding repeating the same response and the same mistakes. More importantly, this deficiency reflects a lack of structural integration— the solution to a problem has not been internalized and is not generalized to new and different situations. Put plainly, "one does not learn from one's mistakes," and makes the same random responses over and over again.

Impulsive Responding. Individuals react impulsively when the control and filtering mechanisms of the processing activities are not performed sufficiently. Therefore impulsive responses are generally partial and/or mistaken. Similar to trial and error responding, there is a lack of structural (internal) integration, and a lack of systematic use of that which has been learned in problem-solving situations (see our discussion of elaboration phase functions in the next section of this chapter). The consequence is a lack of precision and accuracy in responding.

Blocking of Response. This phenomenon is due to a deficiency in the process of regulatory behavior. It often stems from a sharp and sudden transition from unplanned, unrepressed impulsive behavior to behavior that is over-repressed to such an extent that it causes an inability to respond. It reflects, generally, the lack of suitable processing tools for turning the suppression of the response into a thinking activity. It is best responded to, in terms of the application of mediated learning experience, by applying the mediation of feelings of competence and challenge (see Chapter 7 for an explanation of these parameters). In this way, the mediation moves from a sole focus on the emotional aspects of the blocking to a focus on the cognitive strategies required to overcome it.

THE ELABORATION PHASE

In the elaboration phase of the mental act, stimuli are changed by different thinking operations. We sort out the data that has been collected into groups and analyze, compare, create relationships, encode or decode the meaning, create connections between them and other data, summarize, and draw conclusions. In this way we create information and new data that were not included in or go beyond the initial data that was gathered.

A person's ability to extract from reality what is needed to create new things in the world is imparted by means of the mediator. Belongings, objects, and even experiences do not speak to the person in a language of syllogisms and inferences. It is the person who creates the relationships through performing mental operations. One does not receive from nature objects that are classified or time that is divided according to individual needs. One changes the world through a processing system that is imposed on the world.

The elaboration phase is the most flexible stage in the thinking process, even among populations with very low functioning levels, and it may become more accessible among those who have been defined as severely retarded. This flexibility in the central stage of the thinking process reinforces our basic premise concerning the inherent modifiability of human beings by appropriate levels (in terms of quality, intensity, and so forth) of mediated learning experience (MLE). At times it is easier to teach children to process data than to teach them how to collect data, where and how to reflect on them—as based on accurate reception at the input phase—or how to formulate answers properly—as is required in the output phase.

Behaviors at the input and output phases are not always easy to change. On the other hand, surprisingly, it is precisely the elaboration phase—the central stage of thinking that characterizes human beings—that is easier to change. The input and output functions are the product of behavior patterns that the student has formed, and they are often determined by sensory-motor or physiological characteristics (hearing, vision, articulatory skills, and so on). Many of the behaviors that are considered to be without thinking ability can be, in fact, materially improved when linked to elaboration phase functions, thereby improving the functions and processing abilities that show themselves to be stronger and more efficient than manifested without such elaboration phase linking. One of the functions of a dynamic diagnosis, which we will address in the next chapter, is to assess in which of the stages of thinking does the examinee have difficulty, how mediation at one phase affects the others, and so on. For example, has the student not seen what should have been seen, not thought about it, perhaps not seen or thought correctly about it, or is otherwise incapable of formulating the correct or adequate response to it?

Deficient Functions at the Elaboration Phase

Recognizing and Defining the Existence of a Problem. When a student comes up against a contradiction in comparing a certain phenomenon to standards or to other phenomena (either directly experienced or conceptualized), the experience is one of being thrown off balance. What should occur is a sense of a problem. Defining the problem is the initial action in a process designed to restore balance that becomes impaired, following the lack of conformity between the data that has been registered. This is well illustrated in the biblical story of Moses. Moses saw the burning bush, and yet the burning bush was not consumed by the fire. This phenomenon contradicted what Moses considered to be normal: A bush that burns must turn to ash, the bush that was before him was not consumed, and so he went to investigate why the fire did not destroy the bush. What he saw threw him off balance because it was different from what he expected to see, and therefore he deviated from his path in order to restore the sense of balance that he had lost.

This biblical story presents an apt metaphor for the process of responding to a situation that is contrary to what is "known—what can be considered a sense of disequilibrium. Our description in Chapter 5 of William experiencing a dilemma in the museum (and his mother's mediation) and Piaget's problem of the tilted bottles are examples of responding to cognitive disequilibrium. The academic curriculum presents students with many opportunities to confront similar situations. The teacher who mediates engages students in journeys through content that expand and deepen their understanding of the underlying concepts embedded in the content. Take for example the phenomenon of global warming. Why is there controversy among scientists regarding its impact on the environment? What evidence can be gathered regarding its effects? Is it colder in traditionally warm climates? Are there increasing droughts, changes in ocean currents, and the like? Another example comes from our changing view of the structure of the solar system. Long-held understandings of the planets are being re-evaluated. Why is Pluto no longer considered a planet? What is the new evidence? How was it obtained? If it isn't a planet, what is it?

Defining the problem therefore creates in the person an internal motivation to look for a solution and to explain the contradiction or the gap. To perceive the existence of a problem, we must activate a number of cognitive functions such as creating relations between different sources of information, discerning nonconformity or a contradiction between them, and deducing logical contradictions within the information. Those who lack mediation do not feel the lack of balance created following phenomena that apparently testify to a lack of consistency and contradiction in given information. Therefore, awareness of a problem is not created. For example, there are children who can gaze at a picture of a giraffe with a body of a cow and not notice or differentiate a contradiction between the two animals. If they don't notice differences or contradictions they do not formulate a problem. Their curiosity is not aroused; consequently, they do not need to find any explanation and no elaborations or insights are generated.

The phenomenon of the lack of curiosity in children or adults derives in many cases from the same lack of discerning the existence of the problem. Because they do not recognize that there is a problem, their balance is not disturbed, and therefore they have no need to look for solutions. Thus, there is created in them what we term "lack of curiosity" and what is often referred to as a "lack of motivation." So many modern children who are potentially very intelligent often convey that they are quickly bored because of this lack of discernment leading to a lack of curiosity.

To create change in students, we must give them the tools that will enable them to feel the lack of balance in a problematic situation and subsequently to ask questions and to look for answers according to their ability.

The Inability to Distinguish Between Relevant and Irrelevant Data for the Solution of a Problem. The awareness of the very existence of the problem is, as we have mentioned, a precondition for its solution. Once one knows that a problem exists, one must characterize and analyze it to determine the directions one must look for data to resolve it and to decide what data are relevant to the solution. To distinguish between relevant and irrelevant data the use of hypothetical thinking is required. In this cognitive function, we see the close connection to functions at the input phase, including the systematic scanning of stimuli, placing stimuli in time and space, paying attention to multiple sources of information, and so on.

The Episodic Perception of Reality. Episodic perception is manifested by the lack of an inclination to look for and an inability to discern relationships between events, to collect and organize them, and to summarize them. Every event, item, or object is perceived as a one-time event, unconnected to what preceded it or what will follow it. The student who experiences reality episodically expresses a passive attitude toward it; one cannot understand the organization of the events or put them in order by summarizing them, nor can one experience them as a meaningfully integrated whole. Experience is fragmented and cannot be compared or placed into a wider context. At best, such students experience themselves as recipients of information and not as their creator.

The episodic perception of reality results in the production of an extremely poor repertoire of significant cognitive experiences that build high-order ways of thinking and enables a better use of them. A student with an episodic perception does not create relations between stimuli, events, and experiences but remains passive toward them, and thus is unable to learn from them. One does not say to oneself following the experiences: "This happened to me five times. If I focus together on all five times, apart from the differences between them, I can learn from this that when I do X, Y happens to me." Because every event is a new one without any continuity, one does not summarize or learn from the lessons that will enable the drawing of conclusions, and therefore behavior does not change.

The Lack of Spontaneous Comparative Behavior. A spontaneous search for comparison and difference constitutes a necessary and vital condition for the creation of relationships. A spontaneous comparison supplies a constant stream of associations and distinctions between items of information that are stored in our memory, following an encounter with stimuli. Spontaneous comparison is one of the foundation stones of higher-order mental processes.

We stress the spontaneity of the comparison, because those who lack mediation may well be capable of comparing when they are required to or have an internalized need to do so. For example, if children who do not compare are allowed to choose one slice out of two slices of cake, they will compare them in order to receive the bigger slice. This suggests that the mental function of comparison exists and is even activated (under conditions of an internalized need system), but they may not be systematically activated and generalized to the wider world of stimulus responsiveness. That is, the student who is capable of making a comparison between two slices of cake may not necessarily compare two events, two figures, or even two numbers. Thus, the deficiency does not prevent the use of the function but limits it significantly.

A Narrow Mental Field. Complex mental activities demand dealing simultaneously with items of information, some of which we receive from the outside and some of which we must retrieve from memory. Among people with a narrow mental field, the metaphor of the short blanket phenomena applies: when it covers the head, the feet are exposed and vice versa. That is to say, a new item of information that enters the storehouse of memory causes the forgetting of an item of information that was previously learned. This deficient functioning is also connected, like its predecessor, to a person's passive approach to the information. A person who has not been given mediation sees oneself as receiving and transferring information, but not as the creator and the re-constructor of information. There is no belief in the ability to pull out information from memory in a voluntary manner; one does not even remember it in an immediate and spontaneous manner. This deficient function can also be described as a lack of peripheral awareness; one is not aware of aspects of experience that are away from the center of focus and on the edges of what one perceives.

The Lack of Planning Behavior. To plan means to refer to the future and to actions that will be performed in a distant time and place. Deficiencies in planning behavior are liable to be connected to life circumstances—to a reality in which the individual lives from hand to mouth, feels bereft of influence over his or her fate, and therefore does not find any point in planning for the future. Many students with whom we have worked, and who have experienced extreme cultural deprivation or severe disruptions in their lives, as those who survived the Holocaust, often experience an inability to plan ahead and project into the future because of their previous focus on struggling to survive in the immediate here and now, as well as the anxiety and stress that is conjured up when thinking about the future and the lack of models or encouragement to think ahead. The lack of planning also keeps behavioral responses episodic and restricts the development of a wider mental field of awareness.

Lack of Summative Behavior. This is another frequent characteristic of children who have not been given mediation. The child with this cognitive deficiency relates to everything as a separate item or event and does not aggregate them into a unified group or sum them up into an understandable and coalesced phenomenon. This also contributes to an episodic perception of the world. If we were to ask such children how many brothers or sisters they have, they must count them one by one. They do not group separate units into a whole because they have never been asked for or experienced the process of summarization. Cognitively, such situations demonstrate that the whole is truly more than the sum of its parts. When we do not sum up our experience we do not appreciate the holistic nature of our lives.

The Inability to Project Virtual Relationships. As a consequence of a lack of internalization of experience, individuals cannot project to new situations and experiences that do not directly exist in their immediate exposure. Higher-order mental operations and the experience of distancing oneself from immediate and direct experience rely on virtual relationships as an elaboration of direct experience and become an important aspect of perceiving the complexity of the world of stimuli. For example, looking at a picture and projecting actions and feelings stimulated by elements of the picture, such as a ferocious lion devouring its prey, enables the learner to project to other situations like concepts of the food chain and then generalize from this concept to other situations and applications, some of which are far removed from the modality of the direct experience.

Difficulties in Interiorizing. In our description above of virtual relationships, we used the word *project* to indicate the mechanism for forming relationships among objects and events and the need to form inner mental pictures of experiences (the stimulus objects and events). This results in the forming of mental images and representations of that which is experienced. Another term useful to convey this mental act is to transfer to our mind that which we experience through a mechanism of representation. Events, perceptions, and experiences are interiorized through a process of representing them (forming mental pictures, attributing conceptual aspects that link them to one another, and the like), and they become an inseparable part of the cognitive-emotive structure of the person. This is what is meant by interiorization.

Those who have deficient functions in this area are generally limited in their ability to use the principles that were drawn from their experience of learning because they do not form inner pictures or models of what they have learned. Although this difficulty may appear to derive from deficiency of memory, it derives as much from the difficulty of internalizing stimuli. When interiorizing has not taken place, the student needs tangible hints and cannot rely on the information stored in memory. A child who finds it hard to interiorize generally finds it hard to reject or postpone gratification. These difficulties characterize children who have not had access to MLE.

The Lack of Need to Justify Solutions or Responses. The data we have collected at the input phase need to be processed and formulated so that they will be used in arriving at a solution to the problem. An important part of the elaboration phase is for the individual to understand why and how conclusions were reached and to be able to understand the nature of the process of elaboration and problem solving, ultimately conveying to others his or her understanding. In order to be understood by others, the learner must process things so that they will be convincing to him- or herself. Therefore, one must be prepared to give reasons for arguments and feel the need to rationally prove how and why responses were generated.

This need is stimulated as an outcome of mediated learning experience, when the mediator is not satisfied with the student's reply and requires that the learner give reasons for solutions, conclusions, and the processes used to arrive at them. In this sense, this cognitive function is closely related and is a transitional function leading to the output phase. In addressing this cognitive deficiency, the mediator interposes him- or herself between the individual, emphasizing the need to communicate to others and mediating the need to adapt the formulation of solutions so that they will not only be self-understood but be meaningful to others (leading to output phase functions).

THE RELATIONSHIP OF DEFICIENT COGNITIVE FUNCTIONS TO MLE

A student with deficient or defective functions—particularly in the stage of elaboration (processing), but also in other stages—tends to be passive. The student is prepared to carry out the reproduction of the known data but is not prepared to create new information. That is to say, we're not only talking about an intellectual problem, but also about a passive attitude to reality. This kind of passivity sometimes derives from the self-perception as lacking the ability to create information. In such cases the person can only transfer the information that is possessed but not go beyond it.

The three phases of the cognitive activity are not separated but influence one another: the mechanism of the processing is that which dictates to the input stage how, what, and how much to invest in the precise collection of data; similarly, the elaboration phase is influenced by the data that is collected and perceived at the input (reception) phase.

One of the unique components of our perception is the ability to pay attention not only to the outcome but—and perhaps primarily—to the whole thinking process. We do not take the outcomes of an activity as a sole criterion for evaluating performance, but we also consider the process through which the learner arrived at the outcomes.

We can summarize the effect of MLE as providing a whole system of responses in the three phases of the mental act. At the input phase, the mediator imparts to the learner the ability to grasp the data that is required to function in a sharp and comprehensive manner, search for the data systematically, relate to as many sources of information as possible, and use them before conclusions are drawn.

At the elaboration phase, the mediator gives the learner thinking tools that are required to derive benefit from exposure to stimuli. The mediator provides the learner with tools for formulating the problem and may complicate the problem to create the need to add data and to think a little more before reaching a conclusion. The mediator directs the learner to carry out comparative processes and to give rational reasons for his or her conclusions.

At the output phase, the mediator creates in the learner interactive forms of thinking that are completely different from those that would be required if the mediatee did not interact with others. When a person speaks only to him- or herself, or when one is in a dream situation in which the laws of logic have no meaning, there is no need to be interactive. But the need for logic in relating to limits of time and space, the need to summarize things, and the need to classify and arrange them in order are all created because a person is a creature who lives in a society and receives experience through a mediational interaction that is unique to human beings.

MLE is responsible, therefore, for the emergence of the mental operations that enable a student to function efficiently from not only a cognitive standpoint but also from an emotional/energetic perspective, and to communicate with others within the immediate cultural community and beyond. On the other hand, a lack of MLE leads to limitations in social and cultural interaction and causes the appearance of deficient cognitive functions.

We must again stress that we're not talking about an irreversible situation. Exposure to mediation can correct the deficient functions that have been formed because of the absence of previous mediation and modify them significantly.

As an example, we will conclude this chapter by describing a student with whom we worked who presented impulsive behavior that manifested itself by the lack of readiness or inclination to restrain her reactions so that her cognitive development and behavior was significantly impaired, but who responded to MLE.

> Donna was referred to us at the age of 14 with a diagnosis of ADHD. Her failure at school due to a lack of attention and incapacity to restrain her impulsive behavior led to her dropping out of school and associating with other problematic peers who were also academically nonperforming. Her behavior had deteriorated to the point where she was in danger of being at high risk of drug addiction and of preventing the development of academic skills and social relationships. Donna was rebellious and unwilling to accept any discipline imposed on her. She had failed many forms of treatment—both psychological and medical. Mediation for her consisted of the presentation of many tasks (using the Instrumental

Enrichment program) that required her full attention, the coordination of her mental activity, and a persistent search for solutions. At the outset, her responses indicated an absence of the characteristics of ADHD and the ready availability of processes for addressing the tasks and responding appropriately. Donna had many well-established cognitive functions, and those that were fragile or deficient were amenable to mediation through the use of the instruments and a general MLE interaction. She became engaged and involved, began to see herself as competent and able to control her behavior, and became enthusiastic about making changes and seeking more appropriate goals for herself. All of this was reinforced by mediation. Most importantly, Donna was able to observe for herself the available and newly acquired cognitive functions and transfer them outward to her parents, school experiences, and peer relationships.

The mediation of cognitive functions in this case illustrates how the focus on a systematic, positive, and active intervention can modify behavior in significant and sustaining ways. Parents and teachers often attribute such results to "a miracle." Our response is that such changes may truly appear miraculous but are in fact the product of hard work and the use of well-defined and provided interventions—what we have called "man-made miracles."

CHAPTER 10

Dynamic Cognitive Assessment

Earlier in this book we discussed how the theory and concepts of structural cognitive modifiability have been used to develop applications to produce changes. We have now reached a stage in which we must consider a number of practical questions arising from the theory of structural cognitive modifiability (SCM):

1. If a human being is indeed a modifiable creature, as this theory assumes, what is the significance of the conventional and traditional diagnoses using instruments and techniques that are designed to characterize the presumed fixed and unchanging nature of intellectual and cognitive functioning? Given this perspective, can one use them to accurately predict the future development of the individual?
2. If human beings, as they are today, are in fact not the final word and are modifiable, by what means will we be able to bring about change?
3. What are the implications of this modifiability for students as beings who must change not only to the environment, but also for themselves, as they must adapt to new and challenging situations?

We have answered these questions through the development and application of three applied systems that are derived from our theory:

- The first method is that of a dynamic assessment of cognitive functioning and learning potential, the Learning Propensity Assessment Device (LPAD)—a battery of instruments and method of application that focus on the assessment of a human being's modifiability.
- The second method is the Feuerstein Instrumental Enrichment (FIE) program—an instructional curriculum based on a careful delineation of necessary cognitive skills and functions and the incorporation of mediated learning experience methods.
- The third is an application of the Shaping of Mediating Environments (SME). This approach focuses on creating and sustaining the conditions that enable cognitive modifiability to be fulfilled. SME focuses on the creation of an environment that not only facilitates change, but also arouses it.

In this chapter we shall discuss the diagnostic/assessment method we have developed—the dynamic assessment of modifiability using the Learning Propensity Assessment Device (LPAD). This application is based essentially on our answer to the first question posed. Our answer is that, while it is impossible to conclude from measuring the abilities of human beings in the present what their future abilities will or can be, it *is* possible to create samples of the potential for change through the exposure to and observation of specially designed and selected learning activities and to estimate through them a student's learning ability and modifiability.

Because we assume that a human being is capable of modifying itself, this assumption gives rise to the conclusion that a human being is not predictable. Therefore, any attempt to predict in advance a person's development through psychometric methods that measure manifest levels of functioning and that purport to predict the future on the basis of an assessment made under static conditions (at certain stages of life, by certain restricted means, at a particular time and place, and so forth) stands in contradiction to the unpredictable essence of the human being.

THE RATIONALE FOR DYNAMIC ASSESSMENT

The conventional psychometric assessment process cannot predict favorable changes in examinees who function at low levels, nor can it predict who will function at a high level, because modifiability does not take place only in a positive direction. There is the danger of a change for the worse: a deterioration in a person's functioning level. In the wake of sharp criticism (not only ours, but from many sources) of the static approaches to assessment whereby a person is examined at a certain moment in the present and the present behavior is used to predict future behavior and abilities, we have identified and argued for the need of a dynamic approach in assessing human beings' abilities. The need to challenge the psychometric approach came from experience in the 1940s and 1950s, working with the deeply traumatized children of the Holocaust and children with extreme cultural deprivation. For these children the standard psychometric measures were totally inadequate.

Dynamic assessment represents the antithesis of static assessment and thereby challenges the huge examination industry whose major objective is to classify human beings and place them in drawers from which they will never emerge. As mentioned elsewhere in this volume, in the book *The Bell Curve*, Herrnstein and Murray present human beings as unmodifiable entities for whom the cognitive intellectual factor (as measured by IQ tests) is what determines their place in the world. We believe this method has no basis in human reality and essence. It is based on wonderful mathematical means and is convenient, but those who use it fail to take into account the main issue: Human beings have the ability to modify themselves and to be modified in unpredictable ways and directions. Moreover, the new evidence on neuroplasticity strengthens and supports the potential for modifiability (see Chapter 14).

The process of dynamic assessment is designed to assess a human being's propensity for modification, characterizing the way in which the modification is likely to occur in a person, assessing the extent of the possible modification under given conditions, and assessing the significance of the demonstrated modification its implications for adaptability. Perhaps the most important implication of this process is the identification of the appropriate interventions for the particular individual being assessed, as opposed to basing interventions on standardized and normative predictions and, therefore, measuring fixed and unchangeable characteristics.

Those committed to the psychometric approach do not accept the dynamic approach easily. It seems efficient to deal with people as if they are objects that can be measured like something that remains standing where it has been placed—unresisting, unmoving, and not progressing. As scientists, the objective of dealing with questions of the validity of outcomes and their reliability is the discovering of identical outcomes in each and every measurement.

THE DEVELOPMENT OF THE LPAD
AS A DYNAMIC APPROACH TO ASSESSMENT

We began to develop the dynamic approach when we confronted the question of the fate of thousands of children who functioned at a low level at a certain stage in their lives. Had we based our recommendations on their manifest level of functioning at that stage, we would have been obliged to sentence them to lives and forms of functioning that did not at all conform to their true abilities. Therefore, after considerable attempts to use available standard psychometric tools and to adapt them to our populations, we stopped using static tests, which measured them at the unfortunate moments in their lives, and began to develop and use tools that enabled us to estimate the modification that they were liable to attain under appropriate conditions (which we searched for ways of providing).

The Stages of Dynamic Assessment in the LPAD

The learning propensity dynamic assessment (LPAD) is based on three stages, with intervening observation and adaptation between them.

The Pre-Test Phase. In the first stage, which seems like a kind of pretest but in actuality is much more, we examine the current level of functioning in the student by presenting tasks in a variety of selected modalities (stimulus information of a figural, pictorial, verbal, logical/deductive, or numerical nature). The examinee's response is observed and analyzed to determine baseline levels of performance and the types and extent of mediation that should be offered.

The Mediation or Teaching Phase. The second stage is generally a stage of mediated intervention that is intended to teach the learner to cope successfully not only with the specific tasks of the test (including those that were not successfully completed) but also with new tasks. The examiner/assessor, who at this stage fulfills the function of mediator, equips the learner with the thinking tools required to respond to the demands of the task—to identify and define the problem, to gather data, to process data for a solution, and to formulate the solution in a clear and reasoned answer—as determined through observation of the first phase.

The Re-Test Phase. In the third stage, after the intervention of mediation and the mediator's observation and analysis of the effects of the mediation offered on the examinee's response—during which the examinee has been equipped with tools of learning—the examiner presents another task (of a similar nature but with systematically included variations) and essentially repeats the process with the informed observation/analysis that we described above. Here, we ask, how does the learner respond given the learning that has occurred as a consequence of the mediation? To what extent does the learner use it, and is it used properly at the correct time and place?

The process that the learner undergoes enables us to see the extent to which what had previously been inaccessible to the learner has become incorporated within the repertoire of capability. By this method of assessment we are capable of producing not only increased basic skills, but also higher-order thinking functions among examinees who had been considered incapable of coping with them.

Let us take for example the ability to make an analogy—to find the relationship between two objects and to build by means of this relationship a connection between two other objects. An analogy is a vital mental operation that is required in everyday life.

Figure 10.1 presents an exercise adapted from the Raven Progressive Matrices Test, which was developed as a static, psychometric instrument, but which we use as a dynamic test. To create this analogy, the examinee has to find the relation between two figures in the left-hand column or between two of the figures in the first row, and to deduce its relationship to the two figures in the right-hand column or in the second row. To successfully solve this problem, the examinee must formulate the organizing principle behind the relationship between the shapes and use it to complete the missing shape (shape number 4 is the correct response for this problem).

Figure 10.1. One of the Problems from the "B-8 to B-12 Set Variations"

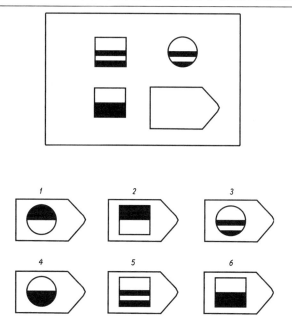

In the example presented, in moving from the left column to the right column the shape remains fixed, whereas its inner content changes according to the principle of reduction. In moving from the first row to the second row, the external shape changes whereas the inner content remains fixed. We teach not only this specific analogy but also the cognitive processes required to create an association and to transfer it (processes of analysis, comparison, preservation of characteristics, synthesis, and so on). The mediator may impart to the examinee two strategies for performing the analogy:

- By categorization—distinguishing the circular family from the squares family and the linear family from the half-filled family.
- According to the transformation principle, distinguishing the circle that changes into a square and two lines that turn into a full half-circle.

When the examinee acquires these two strategies, he or she may apply them in a variety of other situations. Thus, we assess the modifiability of examinees by exposing them to mediated interaction. We impart action principles in a directed, conscious, and clearly formulated manner, and we modify the structure of the thinking while simultaneously examining the type of modification that occurs in it.

In the last stage of the assessment, we check to see how the examinee uses the thought structures that have been created through the mediator to adapt to new situations and solve new problems.

At the beginning of this book we defined intelligence as a human being's dynamic ability to use what is learned in order to adapt to new situations. This is the impulse—the motive—that exists in a human being to be modified. We are interested in assessing intelligence from this standpoint. As we discussed earlier, we are searching not for what human beings know now, but for what they are capable of reaching by means of mediation.

The Essential Differences Between Static and Dynamic Assessment

Dynamic assessment differs from static assessment in four areas: (1) in the assessment tools, (2) in the situation of the assessment, (3) in transferring the emphasis from the product to a process that led to its creation, and (4) in the way of interpreting the obtained results. We shall discuss the differences between the two methods in each of these areas.

1. Differences in the Assessment Tools. The tools of the static assessment are built with the aim of examining a person's levels of knowledge, expertise, and skill. It is expected that the examinee will be capable of responding to them spontaneously, according to the criteria of age and developmental norms that have been established. If, for example, a boy of 12 does not know how to draw a circle, it is assumed that he is an underachiever—that is, at a low level of development for his age. These tools are not intended, and are not capable of, showing the cause of the lack of capability detected in the test.

Static tests are constructed in such a way that no learning will take place. By contrast, dynamic assessment tools are constructed in a way to include situations that are openly intended for learning. A dynamic assessment test is based on the existence of a learning process in its course, because this is the process that we wish to evaluate. Only if learning occurs in the course of the assessment can we locate samples of change and discover the factors that are obstructing change when this does not occur. Therefore, we have created varied assessment tools that enable us to examine the propensity of examinees to learn, to think, and to examine the changes that have taken place in their thinking ability following the assessor/mediator's intervention.

We are not concerned with informational questions that the learner might know. Such questions do not offer the opportunity to modify one's ability to deal with new situations. If, on the other hand, we give the examinee tasks in which he or she is required to perform thinking processes—such as logical operations of addition, subtraction, multiplication, generalization, analysis, synthesis, and so on—we will create conditions of modifiability, performance, and changes that can be observed and registered. These tests deal with what is termed *fluid intelligence*, which can be shaped, as contrasted with *crystallized intelligence*, which does not allow the transfer of the learned principles to new situations. It is this objective that has shaped the system of tools that are included in the LPAD battery of instruments and used at all stages of the mediated intervention.

We observe and analyze the change that takes place in the student, and interpret it as testifying to the existence of propensities/tendencies/readiness whose realization demands a far greater investment of effort than what we can invest in the examinee at the time of the assessment, but which predicts the potential for further and deeper changes. We shall elaborate on the nature of this investment in the next chapter, as we describe the Feuerstein Instrumental Enrichment (FIE) Program.

2. Differences in the Assessment Situations. In static assessment, the role of the assessor is to look for what is fixed, permanent, and unchanging in the learner. The need is to create a standardization of the test conditions, in order to establish its validity and reliability beyond time and the variations in examinees. The situation of the static assessment has to be such that it will be possible to go over it repeatedly in all kinds of places, with all kinds of populations, and by different assessors.

In dynamic assessment, on the other hand, there is no requirement whatsoever for standardization. There are consistent rules and uniform, planned strategies for performing the diagnosis, but because we are comparing the student to him- or herself alone, we do not need (or desire) to make the instructions of the assessment and the interaction between the examiner and the examinee sterile and standard. On the contrary, the assessment situation is constructed and applied so that the differences observed in the performance of the examinee in the different stages of the assessment will have significance. Only if we design the structure of the assessment in this way will we understand why the examinee was unable to solve the problem at the start of the diagnosis, and pinpoint the change that led to success in solving it later.

From the difference in the demand for standardization further differences result. In static assessment, no action must be performed that might cause a change in a person, whereas in the dynamic assessment the assessor must act to bring about change. In dynamic assessment, assessors will do everything in their power to create in the examinee the experience of modifiability. The assessor is in fact an active and involved mediator/teacher. On the other hand, in static assessment, the examiner is required to be passive and remote. The examiner operating from this perspective has to avoid giving any kind of hint to the examinee, even steering clear of giving of feedback about functioning.

The interaction between the examiner and the examinee constitutes an integral part of dynamic assessment. The assessor, being a responsible partner to the success of the student, is interested in the student's success no less than the examinee is. The assessor must arouse in an examinee the aspiration to succeed and must teach how to put the experienced modifiability into practice.

The dynamic assessor, therefore, is not solely an examiner but also a mediator and a teacher who teaches and creates changes. Although assessors have to enable students to respond spontaneously, as in static assessment, they cannot remain content with these responses. As mediators, they must observe the examinee and identify the deficient functions, those that cause difficulties in functioning. They must direct interventions toward repairing them and equip students with the tools required to modify functioning (and themselves).

This difference in the role of the examiner influences the degree of motivation of examinees to perform what is asked of them in the course of the assessment and the relationship between themselves and the assessor. In static diagnosis, examinees often experience feelings of suspicion, performance tension, and fear of the trap that the testing process is setting for them. In the framework of dynamic assessment, these feelings change completely—in many cases students emerge after quite a few hours of assessment with a sense of ability that they never experienced before. After observing these changes, parents of children assessed in a dynamic approach often asked us: "What drug did you give my child?" They cannot conceive that the mediated interaction is what has so affected their child's feeling of capability and his or her self-image.

It should be pointed out that we are assessing not only children but also adults and getting the same types of reaction to being assessed in this manner. Very intelligent and well-functioning adults at times require a dynamic assessment of their ability to learn and to adapt to new situations.

Changes in the test situation involve a large variety of interventions affecting the nature of the interaction. For example, in the psychometric approach, giving the learner information regarding what caused success or failure, identifying what was learned or changed in responses to the test, and the like are either totally forbidden or greatly discouraged because these are seen as potential challenges to the reliability and validity of the procedures. In stark contrast, the structure of the instruments and the expectations of interaction in the LPAD/dynamic assessment approach are specifically designed to provide just such feedback.

3. Changing the Emphasis from a Product to a Process Orientation. In dynamic assessment, we shift the focus from the outcomes of the tests to a focus on the process that the student undergoes in the course of the assessment. We ask the question: What is the process that made the examinee succeed or fail? Is it in the input or output phase functions (more peripheral components), or is it in the elaboration phase (more central to processing functions)? Answers to these questions will determine the extent and nature of the mediation offered in the assessment.

The conventional assessor will say: "I want to know what you know and what you don't know, what you achieved at a certain time and what you didn't succeed in achieving in this time. Even if you know the answer but didn't arrive at it in the time allocated, this knowledge is not significant from my standpoint." If the examinee asks a question the examiner will not answer. The conventional static orientation to the examinee is: "You are here in order to answer questions, not in order to ask questions." On the other hand, the dynamic assessor asks: "What is the process through which the examinee can be modified? How can we bring about change in him or her?" We are looking for signs of change, representing differences between pre-testing and post-testing. We teach a principle and want to know how the examinee will use it in a new situation that demands the ability to adapt to change. For example, if I have taught the examinee to perform formal analogies in a verbal modality, I will assess how the examinee uses what has been learned in coping with a problem that presents numerical analogies.

In this situation, we are interested in knowing not only whether the examinee has learned the task, but also where and how what has been learned can be applied (generalized) to other areas of functioning, with higher levels of difficulty and differences in format, required operations, and so on.

This change means that the dynamic assessment process does not produce or emphasize numerical scores, other than indicators of initial (baseline) and after mediation levels of performance. The desired and useful outcome of dynamic assessment is the production of a profile of modifiability. This profile is a narrative description of the nature of the cognitive functions employed, the types of mediation offered, and the changes elicited.

4. Differences in Interpretation of the Outcomes of Assessment. In static assessment the outcomes of tests are summed up in quantitative terms (the number of correct answers as against the number of incorrect answers). They are then analyzed statistically, relative to the norms constructed according to the results of examinees considered to be of a comparable nature (from the standpoint of their age and other variables). On the other hand, the outcomes of dynamic assessment are not interpreted in the basis of statistically derived indices (averages, percentiles, standard scores, etc.), which we consider to be an artificial outcome made up of all kinds of data whose level of importance differs and, most importantly, do not express the being of the student. Put another way, if the goal of assessment is to uncover the individual's learning potential and to address ways in which learning can be facilitated to manifest real learning potential, using normative and statistically derived comparisons will obscure such a perspective to the great disadvantage of the learner. In dynamic assessment, in contrast, we locate the high points of the functioning of the student and according to them we conclude what lies beneath the surface—the abilities that are not given expression that we must reveal and develop. We examine not only the solution of the examinee but also the reasons for the solution that were chosen—the reasoning behind the choice of one or another answer. We are looking for the buds of the change, and see in them a confirmation of the examinee's ability to continue to be modified, and try to define the conditions required to achieve additional changes. We are reminded of a metaphor developed by Jastak, who said that if you want to know the capacity of a vessel, you cannot measure it periodically and sum up the mean of your measurements. You must "fill it to capacity" to know its potential volume.

So it is with the learner's cognitive capacity. You must literally fill him or her up to know what can be achieved.

THE COGNITIVE FUNCTIONS AND THE COGNITIVE MAP

We analyze the findings of the assessment with the aid of two conceptual systems that enable us to describe the processes responsible for the examinee's functioning, to locate them, and to guide our observations and subsequent mediational interventions. These have been described in earlier chapters and will be reviewed here to put them into the context of assessment.

The Deficient Cognitive Functions

We want to know why the examinee, who at times can be seen to think well, fails every time. Why is an incorrect answer given when it seems to us that there is a capability of giving a correct answer? Is there difficulty in formulating the answer at the output phase? Or perhaps sufficient data has not been gathered or has not been processed properly at the input phase or represents a failure to solve the problem due to deficiencies at the elaboration phase. If so, we are interested in identifying the deficient functions in the examinee's performance and locating the stage in the mental act that needs repairing. The cognitive deficiencies describe the conditions responsible for the learner's response—its nature, quality, and so on.

The Cognitive Map

The Cognitive Map is a conceptual tool that describes the dimensions of the task believed to be responsible for the failure of the individual to respond adequately. It enables us to analyze the cognitive characteristics of every task. The map comprises seven variables, according to which we characterize the demands made on the examinee by a given task to understand the causes of failure or success, according to the extent in which the examinee manages to cope with its demands. There are seven variables for analyzing a task:

1. The content world the task deals with and the learner's familiarity with it.
2. The modalities of the task. That is to say, the language in which the task is presented and in which the answer has to be expressed, such as verbal, formal, numerical, and pictorial modalities. A task can be made up of one or a combination of several modalities.
3. The predominant thinking phase on which the performance of the task is focused: the input, elaboration, and output. For example, if the performer is required to draw, the task is focused on the output phase. If the examinee is asked to identify a triangle in a cloud of dots, the task is focused on the input phase.

4. The main thinking (mental) operation required to perform the task, such as classification, making comparisons, formulating analogies, creation of series, inductive and deductive thinking, and so on.
5. The level of abstraction of the task content, as a function of the degree of distance between the performer's direct concrete experience and the object reflected in the task. For example, when I touch an object or see it with my own eyes, the interaction occurs at zero distance. When I call the object by name, the level of abstraction is higher. When I say "two tables" I am not referring to a given table as an object with a singular existence, but to the concept "table," which brings the object into a group that is comprised of other objects that have a shared identity. When I say "furniture" I am already located at a great distance, because I give the table a group association that does not exist in reality but in my conceptual system. The abstraction is therefore an indicator of the distance from the object that the person's thinking action is capable of attaining. It is an interesting and important paradox that when we go up a level of abstraction, as in viewing the ground from the height of an airplane, we are no longer able to see the differences among phenomena, but we begin to consider the common features that identify them.
6. The level of complexity of the task—the number of units of information from which it is formed, their scope, and the level of novelty of the information. For example, when the performer is required to know what will be the next number in a series of numbers arranged according to a combination of two organizing principles, a complex task must be performed, but if the series of numbers rises by a consistent relationship to one another, then the level of complexity of the task is far lower.
7. The level of efficiency required for performing the task. Efficiency is defined according to three traits: the speed required for performing the task, the accuracy required to perform it, and the sense of effort accompanying the performance of the task. Whereas the first two traits are measurable, the last one depends on the perception of the learner. The level of accuracy and the speed required for performing the task often determine the level of effort required of the performer and the relative ease with which the task will be performed. The more skilled in performing the action, the higher the level of efficiency will be required. But it should be pointed out that the level of efficiency may be influenced by difficulties in one of the other variables of the cognitive map.

Therefore, every task deals with a certain content. It is presented in certain modalities. It demands the activation of one or more of the phases of thinking. It requires the activation of thinking operations. It possesses a certain level of complexity and abstraction and requires a certain level of efficiency to perform it properly. We are assisted by the cognitive map to systematically analyze tasks, not only in dynamic assessment, but in every area—

including regular learning tasks—and also for analyzing the Instrumental Enrichment tasks, which we shall deal with in the next chapter.

These two conceptual tools—the list of the deficient cognitive functions and the cognitive map—help us analyze the thinking processes of examinees as they cope with tasks in the course of the assessment and to draw conclusions on how we can modify them.

To conclude our discussion about dynamic assessment and to show how the principles of the assessment are applied in practice in the assessment instruments, we present tasks from two of the LPAD tests.

TASK 1: A FORMAL (SHAPES) ANALOGY

To arrive at the correct answer for the problem presented in Figure 10.2 (answer 4), the examinee must identify the principle of the change (from the top to the bottom: a reduction of the external shape; from left to right, a change of the external shape) and the principle of preservation (from top to bottom: a preservation of the inner space). Choice of any one of the other answers (the incorrect ones) testifies to a deficient cognitive function, such as: a restricted mental field, difficulty in referring to more than one variable at the same time, difficulty in performing an analogy, and so forth.

Figure 10.2. Task D-5 from "Set Variations B8-B12"

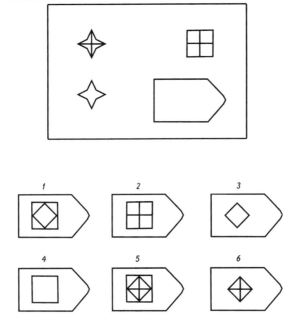

TASK 2: A VERBAL ANALOGY IN THE AREA OF TIME CONCEPTS

In the problem presented in Figure 10.3, the examinee is requested to identify the principle whereby the concept "minute" relates to the concept
"hour," and to project it on the relation between the second pair of concepts; "minute" relating to "hour" as "month" relates to "year" (answer 6
is the correct answer). In this task four of the six possibilities of the answer
relate to time, but only one of them (answer 6) expresses the analogy principle on which the question is based. On the other hand, answer 2 ("good")
has no connection with the analogy. A student that chooses this answer is
looking perhaps for associative connections between the words. The student
who chooses answer 5 ("fat") might have a language difficulty, is confusing
words or acting impulsively, or perhaps is experiencing blurred perception.

Figure 10.3. Task C9 from the "Tri-Modal Analogies Test"

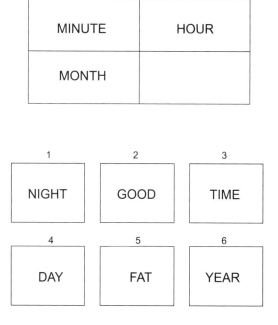

To summarize briefly, these two examples show how in dynamic assessment we are not satisfied only with the student's answer but must orient
our approach and the construction and presentation of tasks to inquire into
the factors that contribute to the student's responses, which lead to the
development of interventions (mediation) that are meant to increase the
potential for performing adequately.

CHAPTER 11

Creating Structural Cognitive Change: The Feuerstein Instrumental Enrichment (FIE) Program

After we have assumed the existence of modifiability in students and all human beings and have assessed their modifiability, we are now ready to address our next question: If a person is indeed modifiable, how do we create the conditions of modifiability? It is the answer to this question that is the impetus for our second applied method that is drawn from mediated learning—the Feuerstein Instrumental Enrichment (FIE) program. The term *instrumental* denotes a process that applies specially designed tools to mediate the acquisition of enhanced cognitive functions.

We began to build the system of instruments in approximately 1957. It was intended to mediate to the person the processes required to improve learning ability and to derive the maximum benefit from exposure to a variety of tasks that required the use of mental operations. With the help of the instruments, we want to create in learners the thinking structures and emotional motivations that will enable them to modify themselves in the course of direct contact with information, stimuli, and experiences.

It is no secret that more than a few children leave school like the fox that left the vineyard in the fable: thinner than when he went in. They do not absorb what is learned and, even if they do, they do not use what they have learned to adapt to new situations. It is a sad reality that most educational systems still set the transmission of knowledge as the major goal of instruction instead of emphasizing the development of thinking. There are at least two major problems with this emphasis on knowledge transmission, as we view it: There are many differences between students with regard to their ability to use the knowledge that they receive to adapt to new situations, and the facts that are learned will soon be obsolete in the fast-changing world of content and required skills. FIE, on the other hand, is aimed at creating the mental functions in human beings that are prerequisites for learning and fostering the development of strategies to benefit from learning.

By this method we are focusing on changing learners and ultimately the fundamental educational systems in which they learn—the teachers, the organizational structures, and eventually even the instructional materials (see Chapter 13). We ask the question, Can we modify learners so that they will derive benefit not only from optimal learning situations, but also from less successful instructional materials or from a teacher who does not give the learner what is required to succeed? Our answer, which we elaborate on in Chapter 13, is that we do not content ourselves with only a modification of the student, but with the necessity for a broader focus on the structure of the educational system in which learning occurs. The provision of FIE responds to these issues but cannot stand alone.

In this regard, we are concerned also about modifying the teachers' beliefs about learning potential and its modifiability, as well as their frameworks for teaching students (i.e., the processes and content of learning). We believe, and have experienced in practice, that as teachers are exposed to the theories of SCM and MLE along with the FIE program, they teach differently in their curriculum areas and relate differently to students—whether or not they are actively teaching FIE.

The source of the power of FIE is its theoretical basis—applying the theory of structural cognitive modifiability (SCM) and mediated learning experience (MLE). From their principles we have drawn the structure of the instruments, their contents, and the ways of mediation that accompany their activation.

THE INSTRUMENTS OF FIE AND THE PRINCIPLES OF THEIR USE

FIE represents the built-in application of the mediated learning method. It is, in fact, a program of mediated interaction that is carried out in the framework of a system of tasks and exercises. The program has two levels: FIE Standard, comprised of 15 instruments that are transmitted in a classroom context for 3 to 5 hours per week over a period of 2 to 3 years, according to the level of the learners and their functioning; and FIE Basic, currently comprised of 11 instruments. The Basic is designed for children from ages 3 or 4 to approximately age 7, and also for the very low functioning older learner. It is currently in a state of further development and additional instruments are expected to be added to the program over time. (Chapter 13 further elaborates on the FIE–B.)

The program is transmitted to the learner by a teacher/mediator who is well trained in the application of the program, who believes in learners' modifiability and the need to help them with this, and who understands the central role of thinking in the development of modifiability.

We prefer teaching in a classroom group environment to individual teaching because the classroom makes possible a greater mediated intensity to that which is transmitted in interaction between two people. The pupils mediate one to another and the teacher mediates the students and adds qualitative interaction in the classroom.

The instruments themselves mediate to the one who performs the tasks included in them. They are constructed such that the learners arrive at an awareness of their thinking processes in the course of performing the tasks. At the same time, the tasks cannot stand on their own as a work instrument for the pupil. The instruments place the learner in situations where help must be accepted. Even adults who will not under any circumstances agree that someone else should "stir the tea for them" find themselves requesting assistance when working with the enrichment instruments.

The Structure of the Instruments

The enrichment instruments deal with different aspects of relationships. The instruments are built as individual lessons that are gradually compiled into integrated work notebooks or portfolios that can be referred to and reviewed. They contain mainly pen-and-pencil tasks that are presented in different modalities—figural, verbal, pictorial, and numerical. The instruments deal in a focused manner with relationships because, in our opinion, understanding a relationship represents a basis for developing the type of abstract, creative, and flexible thinking required to obtain structural cognitive modification.

Each instrument is focused on a primary aspect of relationships: for example, the *Analytic Perception* instrument deals with the relation between the whole and its part; the *Syllogisms* instrument focuses on the relations between groups. Other instruments deal with relationships of time, space, size, family, and so forth. There are often secondary associations and concepts that are experienced as the primary relationships are encountered.

The enrichment instruments are intended for activating the cognitive functions required for developing thinking and learning ability. Each instrument begins with relatively simple tasks, although intelligent adults are also liable to find themselves having to invest effort to perform them properly. Gradually, the tasks become increasingly complex, requiring intensive activation of the mental processes in the phases of input, elaboration, and output. The tasks of the instruments are selected, designed, and directed toward the development of systematic thinking and learning skills that activate and repair (if needed) the learner's deficient cognitive functions.

The instruments present a generalized learning content, and therefore there is minimal demand for specific previous knowledge required to work in them. However, performance of the tasks obliges the learner to activate and use cognitive functions. We shall illustrate these qualities with examples from several instruments.

Examples from Several Instruments

Transitive Relations. The transitive relations that the learner has to discover are formulated in the schema of the task shown in Figure 11.1: If A + B = C + D, and A = D, what will be the relation between B and C?

The learner must perform transitive thinking; that is, transfer knowledge from place to place and create new knowledge from knowledge that has been transferred.

Figure 11.1. An Example from "Transitive Relations"

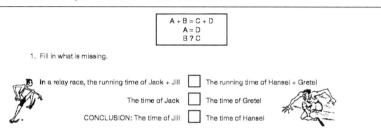

Comparison. In the example shown in Figure 11.2, the learner is required to compare two drawings and to point out what is common to them (riding), and what is different between them (the objects that are being ridden). The demand to formulate the comparison in a single word is aimed at making the learner attain a higher conceptual standard: recognizing the common denominator of the two riders on the horse and on the bicycle and extrapolating the concept of riding. The act of comparison gives the learner the ability to extract from the data new information that was not given in the question.

Figure 11.2. An Example from "Comparisons"

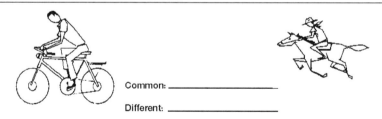

Organization of Dots. In the example shown in Figure 11.3, the learner is required to identify in a cloud of dots two squares and a triangle, according to the example given on the left-hand side. A correct perception in itself is not sufficient to find these shapes. The ability to perform representation is required—to imagine in one's mind what will happen to the model if it is turned around, if the triangle is placed next to the square and its position is changed.

Figure 11.3. An Example from "Organization of Dots"

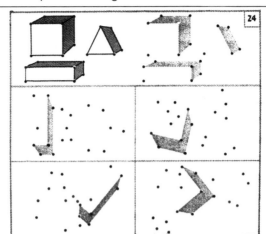

These examples illustrate how the instruments improve learning ability. The student learns where and how to look for data, how to formulate a principle, how to determine what is expected but does not yet exist, and how to define goals and achieve them. In this instrument, cognition is put in the service of helping the perception—we have used the metaphor of providing "cognitive crutches for limping perception."

The Content of the Instruments

The contents of FIE are designed to activate thought processes. When we ask the learner to connect points and find geometrical shapes in a field of dots, it is clear that this task has content. But this content is only a means of activating thinking processes. We are interested in awakening the learner's desire to plan, repress impulses, and find virtual relations between objects that exist solely by virtue of the organization that is introduced into them. Consequently, the content has no significance in itself; it is only a means to achieve our aims.

The Learning Objectives of the Program

The method embedded in the instruments and the presentation of lessons teaches the learner to think and to utilize thinking strategies without being limited by knowledge of a certain subject or basing oneself on it as a source of knowledge. This stands in contrast to other programs in which thinking ability is developed while imparting knowledge in specific content areas (known as *domain specific* knowledge), such as mathematics, geography, literature, or any other study subject. It is our view that the functions of gathering data and elaborating on it will be very helpful in the content areas. Devoid of these skills, learning content will be inefficient and perhaps impossible.

THE AIMS OF FIE: SUBGOALS TO REACH THE MAIN GOAL

The Main Goals of the Program

The main aim of the FIE program is to increase a person's modifiability. To derive benefit from learning opportunities of any kind, the pupil must be capable of learning from experiences, whether they were created intentionally to develop thinking or occurred by themselves as experiences to which they were exposed in everyday life.

The ability to learn and to derive benefit from learning does not exist to the same degree in each one of us. There are people who derive benefit from any exposure, random or intentional. Others are limited in their ability to derive benefit from learning opportunities. When we are exposed to many experiences and stimuli, even very powerful ones, we may be only minimally influenced by them, if at all.

The ability to learn is a skill that demands development in all of us, no matter our intelligence or previous level of performance. It is not innate, as has been commonly presumed. Which one of us has not come across ordinary pupils or even gifted ones who are not capable of distinguishing between the data that are relevant to the task they are engaged in and the data which are not? And this is not a function of socioeconomic status; everyone experiences helplessness when exposed to advanced demands for performance or responding. Such situations reach their height in those countries that impose matriculation examinations on their graduating students. It is difficult to meet such demands without developing the cognitive ability to learn.

Therefore, FIE is also designed for people with high levels of functioning who need to improve their modifiability in order to adapt to the swift changes taking place around them. In fact, this method has been used in many high-tech industries in France (at SNECMA, Peugeot, Renault, and others) and the United States (at Motorola). The aim of these projects was to equip workers with additional thinking strategies to those that they already possess, so they could adapt to the increasing demands being made on them in the context of their work in the industries.

Those who find it difficult to learn require not only the ability to process stimuli but also a factor that will help to make the stimuli meaningful to them. They need to develop the tendency to exploit the stimuli in order to accumulate experience and to shape themselves through it, and they must be more flexible from a cognitive point of view and develop schemata of thinking that allow them to hold an interaction with new data. They also must learn new ways of perception, of processing, and responding. This includes (in the terms of Piaget) assimilation of what is new and more complex, and crystallization by the selfsame process of assimilation in the direction of accommodation and adaptation to the new situations. Thus the ability of the person with learning difficulties to learn and derive benefit from experiences will be increased.

The Subgoals

To achieve the major goal of the program, we have defined six subgoals by which we have designed the tasks, reflecting the didactic principles according to which we expose the program to students. The tasks and the structure of FIE also incorporate the special relations between the teacher/mediator and the pupil/mediatee—the provision of MLE.

Subgoal 1: To correct deficient cognitive functions. What has been previously presented as a condition for learning is now described as a subgoal. In a more concrete manner, we are interested in correcting the deficient cognitive functions that we have identified by dynamic assessment in the LPAD, or through initial observations of student responses to FIE instruments. Our focus is on those functions that are responsible for the limited learning abilities and modifiability of the learner.

The tasks are constructed so as to require activation of the cognitive functions to perform them. At the time when the students encounter difficulty in coping with the task, their deficient functions are exposed. They become aware of them as they do not succeed in solving the problem—perhaps due to a lack organization, not gathering data accurately, working unsystematically, or the lack of other relevant and needed cognitive functions.

For example, in the task from the instrument *Organization of Dots*, which we presented above, the action of separating a given figure from within a cloud of dots demands regulation of behavior, suppression of some information, control of impulsiveness, and preservation of constants—that is, the preservation of the figure and its identification despite the change in its position, and despite its being concealed within a shapeless cloud of dots. To perform this task, the learner's perception has to be much more exact than in a situation in which there is no need to isolate what we are looking for among a larger number of stimuli. The performer of the task has to develop efficient search strategies and to use cognitive processes to solve the problem.

In one's search for the concealed figure (in the above case with two squares and a triangle), the performer has to gather more exact information about it—to compare the traits of the square to those of the triangle or the rectangle to distinguish between them. For this quantitative criteria to be used—for example, in the number of sides and the number of angles—concepts such as distance and length must be employed. To identify the shape when its direction is different, one must also be capable of preserving constants. To find the figure within a cloud of dots one has to make virtual relationships and so on.

The gaps built into the task create in the learner a situation of cognitive dissonance, and this situation awakens a need to activate the processes required to arrive at the solution—that is, to close the gaps and restore the balance.

The outcomes of the learner's actions make possible immediate feedback, which enables the correction of mistakes and creates a greater readiness to suppress impulsiveness, to rebuild assumptions, and to arrive at the correct solution. FIE is so programmed that it will confront the learner with the stimuli, experiences, and tasks that correct the specific deficient functions.

Subgoal 2: To impart or improve a system of basic concepts and basic thinking operations. The existence of basic concepts like *square, triangle, center, before, after, identical, similar,* and *different* constitute a condition for the performance of the generalizations required for the transfer of learning. But these concepts are not always available to the learner, and we must impart them as a prerequisite for learning. Also thinking operations like analogy, comparison, logical multiplication, and subtraction must be a part of the learner's repertoire of cognitive abilities. These concepts require a verbal denotation—the learner may know what an analogy is but not be able to label and generalize from it as an operational concept applied to other tasks and situations.

This subgoal is achieved mainly through the active intervention of the teacher/mediator, who imparts to the learner the concepts and thinking operations required to carry out the task in line with its specific requirements. Consider the example in Figure 11.4. To perform this task, the learner has to be familiar with the concepts of size, shape, and direction and also follow the directions utilizing their conceptual familiarity.

Subgoal 3: To impart the ability to generalize and transfer of what is learned. The structuring of the learner's inclination to generalize and to transfer the knowledge acquired to a new situation constitutes a central objective of learning. This subgoal, which is often neglected in many programs, is achieved mainly through the creation of an insight in learners about their thinking processes and giving them immediate opportunities to put them into practice. The mediator/teacher is not content to simply direct learners to arrive at the solution of the certain problem, but helps them to understand the thinking process they have gone through in order to arrive at the solution. The mediator analyzes the process with the learners, makes them conscious of it, and also enables them to arrive at the insight: "Ah, ha! I can use the method I used here in another place."

Figure 11.4. An Example from "Instructions"

The forms are arranged on the line in size order.

The orange shape is larger than the _____ shape and _____ than the white shape.

The largest shape is on the _____ side.

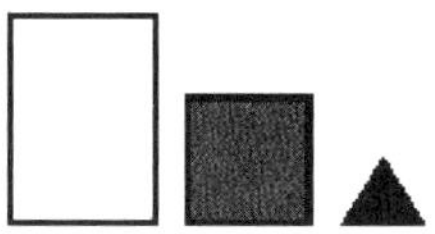

Insightful thinking enables the learner to understand that functions activated in a given task are also relevant to other tasks. Insight directs learners to discover the changes that have taken place in their own cognitive structure. These changes will constitute a source for new strategies that will be implemented in other and different situations from those that they have already been exposed to.

Insightful learning, which leads to generalization and the transfer of what is learned, is intimately connected to the concept of transcendence, which is defined as a parameter of MLE (as we discussed in Chapters 5 and 6). The relationship of the mediator with the learner is not only directed at the success of the present task but to looking ahead at tasks that will be responded to in the future.

Many programs do not succeed in bringing the learner to generalization and to transference, because they are based on the assumption that they take place spontaneously in the learner, as if they are derived solely from within the person. FIE, in contrast, actively promotes the development of generalizations through the tasks of the instrument and how they are mediated, starting with the structure of the instruction—explicitly emphasizing the acquisition and use of concepts.

The rules, principles, strategies, customs, and habits that were acquired are transferred by the learner to areas that are not directly or immediately connected to the initial task through a process that we call *bridging*. In the bridging process, the mediator directs the learner constantly to search for situations whose points of similarity make it possible to apply the same principle to them. Transfer is ensured through the learner's tendency to compare situations, discover their points of difference and similarity, refer to the experience that has accumulated in solving problems in similar situations, and choose a strategy that has proved useful in the past to resolve a new problem. In this way, the learner utilizes the learned mental operations and thinking strategies. This subgoal can be illustrated through a task from the instrument *Organization of Dots*, as shown in Figure 11.5.

Figure 11.5. A Task from "Organization of Dots"

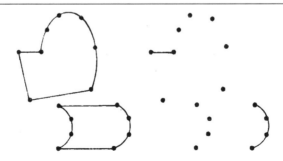

After one has interiorized the shapes (square and triangle) in the first pages of the instrument, the learner is required to transfer the strategies learned (such as analyzing the shape of the figure, the number of sides, the relationship between them, the angles, and so forth) and to use them in a new and more complex task involving curved, irregular shapes.

Subgoal 4: To develop extrinsic motivation. The source of the learner's motivation to apply what has been learned can be extrinsic, like responding to the demands of the teacher/mediator or seeking rewards received for performing tasks, as occurs with regard to many of our everyday tasks. At the same time, our goal is also to develop the learner's sources of inner motivation because there is not always a clear and immediate connection between the performance, the demands, and the rewards, and the desire to perform cannot be exclusively dependent on them.

Many programs lack an appeal to an intrinsic motivational source. This is particularly important for those students with learning difficulties or histories of prior failure in learning situations. A person who experiences learning difficulties is generally a realist who wants to learn only that which will bring immediate benefit. The higher-order thinking processes are of little interest. Therefore, how are we going to create intrinsic motivation for functioning that does not answer a tangible, real, and immediate need?

We try to produce intrinsic motivation by a two-stage process: In the first stage, which is aimed at achieving the subgoal that we are describing here, we direct our mediation to the arousal of an interest in the task, the will to perform it, and an awareness of the ability to succeed with it—and then attach to it clearly related and relevant benefits and rewards for successful fulfillment. This is still dependent on an external source—in the particular nature of the task and the requirements to respond to it—but it is connected to the performance itself—and then related to a third factor—the achieving of success and a related reward.

In the second stage, which is designed to achieve the next subgoal, we develop in the learner an intrinsic motivation to learn and to perform the tasks—namely, a will to perform that is not conditioned by the way in which the task and interactions around it are designed and rewarded.

Here we must point out the differences between this approach and programs that are based on pure behavioral modification, such as the ABA program popular in the United States and elsewhere. In the latter, there is no attempt to link behavioral outcomes to internal states of change or to focus learners away from the overt reinforcers to gain personal meaning in the task accomplishment for its own sake—moving from extrinsic to intrinsic motivation. We see this as a serious limitation in such programs, for reasons that we outline here and in that which follows.

For learners to want to perform a task it has to attract and interest them. We achieve this by means of tasks that are mentally difficult and complex, and with which the learner copes with the aid of appropriate mediation. After learners have succeeded in performing the task with the help of the mediator, they are encouraged to carry on working independently—through the structure of the FIE lesson and the emphasis on bridging.

The tasks in the program are built so that all learners—including those with learning difficulties as well as high functioning learners, and also the teachers themselves must invest effort in them. The program presents a challenge for everyone because the tasks' complexity arises from the mental activity required to perform them and not from any prior knowledge.

We shall illustrate the development in the degree of complexity of tasks from the instrument, *Numerical Progressions*.

Figure 11.6. Tasks from "Numerical Progressions"

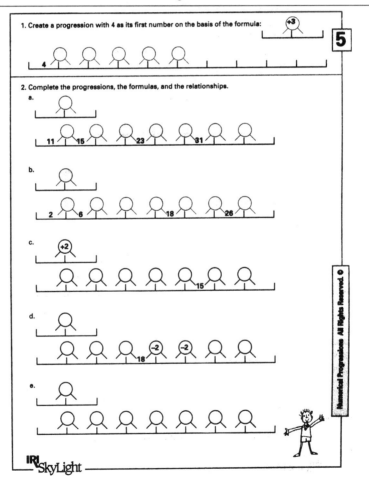

From a relatively simple depiction of relationships, the learner must solve progressions of differing and increased complexity, analyzing the numerical relationships and the way they are schematically portrayed.

Motivation arising from the very interest that the task arouses in the learner is meaningful, both from the standpoint of performance of the task as well as from a social standpoint. Regarding the task itself, the significance lies in the will (at times even a fierce desire) to perform the mental operations that the task demands. From a social standpoint, because performing the task requires interaction with the teacher/mediator and peers, many children who are constantly faced with failure in the classroom learn through their exposure to the structure and presentation of FIE that they are able to succeed exactly like the good pupils in the class.

Enjoyment of the classroom situation represents, as a rule, an entirely new feeling for those with learning difficulties, whose primary experience has been only frustration and disappointment.

Teachers and pupils find themselves very close to one another when they perform the enrichment tasks because they demand investment of effort from everyone. Thus, the dynamic interaction of the three partners to MLE (teacher/mediator, task, and pupil) becomes much more equilateral than in other learning situations. Pupils are given an opportunity to succeed and feel capable in areas where even adults have to make an effort to succeed, and learners are attracted to tasks that change their status with such great effectiveness.

Those who learn according to the program do not receive evaluative grades or marks but derive from it a sense of personal achievement, which is more important to them than a mark given by a teacher. However, many students start to experience improvements in their academic functioning, which they often (insightfully) attribute to their FIE experience.

Subgoal 5: To create intrinsic motivation by the consolidation of thinking habits. After we have improved thinking ability, imparted ways of thinking, and aroused the will to learn the program, we have to ascertain that all that has been acquired through it will not fade with time through lack of use but will become an intrinsic and thus a permanent need.

We create in the learner a permanent need to perform in this way and not another way by turning the desired way of performance into a habit. A habit is a source of intrinsic motivation of behavior—when we are used to doing something we do it not because it is necessary at this moment but from our accustomed way of responding.

The creation of habits is considered as being opposed to learning through discovery, in a spontaneous and flexible approach. Therefore, many learning programs largely tend to neglect and even oppose the structuring of thinking habits. They require the learner to apply a principle that has been learned in a specific situation and immediately go on to learn another principle. No attempt is made to create or consolidate thinking habits.

The building of habits usually requires more time than that required in a regular learning syllabus in which principles and rules are learned in a hit and run manner. To create a learning habit, intensive activity is needed—if I do gymnastic exercises once in 3 months, the habit of physical activity will not develop in me, but it will develop if I do exercises 3 times a week (and begin to feel the positive effects).

A habit is created, therefore, by repetition. But repetition in itself is experienced as monotonous, mechanical, and as not requiring thinking processes. In FIE we repeat the task, retaining the basic principle but providing a systematically structured variation. The learner performs many repetitions, but never of exactly the same exercise, experiencing variations of it. We take care to leave one or two parameters constant but change all the other parameters, and so we change the data of the problem while preserving the thinking processes required for its solution. In this way the habit is not created at the expense of the development of the ability to cope with new problems. The learner finds in every task a combination of familiar elements and actions that are repeated, together with new elements that complicate the task or enrich it, elements that must be discovered despite a familiarity with the problem. This requires the individual to adapt to the inventiveness of the task.

The technique that we use to create habits is based on Piaget's accommodation and assimilation processes that we described above. We create in the learner a thinking schemata through repetition of those behaviors, and then, for the schemata to absorb within it new elements, we create conditions that preserve its flexibility. A flexible habit is created, therefore, by means of adaptive repetitiveness. The habit is produced with regard to orientation, principle, and the activation of a thinking process, and under no circumstances with regard to a certain determined solution.

If I wish to watch the flight of a bird, for example, will I use glasses or binoculars? Our aim is not to accustom the learner to always choose glasses, obviously, but to create the habit of considering what to use and to make choices that conform to the situation in question—do I want to see the details of the bird up close, or rather observe the panorama of the bird in flight? That will determine the choice of what I use to look at the bird. We illustrate controlled repetitiveness by means of a task from the instrument *Orientation in Space I*, as shown in Figure 11.7.

This task is intended to get the learner to interiorize the relativity of the directions in which the various objects are found and described in relation to the person contemplating them. The principle of relationship is applied again and again in every component of the task, but the data change and the form of the question also changes.

The need to consolidate the cognitive processes that have been acquired is especially marked in the output and input phases of the mental act, in which there exists a greater resistance to change than at the elaboration phase. Therefore, they demand a greater investment to attain a higher level of automatization and efficiency. For instance, if we desire to cause a learner with a blurred perception to invest effort to sharpen and clarify it, we must provide many situations that will force sharpening of perception. This is also the case in the output phase: Understanding the term *impulsiveness*, for example, is not sufficient to suppress it. First of all, we have to neutralize the habit of responding impulsively, and the best way to get rid of a habit is to replace it with another more desirable habit—"let's respond slowly and carefully so that you will be understood!"

One can explain the rise in effectiveness of FIE found in the research of Rand and others (1981) at least partly by the process of consolidation and shaping of the thinking habits of the learner—habits that time and repetition reinforce.

Figure 11.7. Task from "Orientation in Space-I"

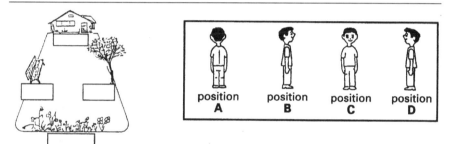

I. On which side of the boy is the object?

Position		Object	Side of person
1.	B	House	
2.	C	Flowers	
3.	A	Flowers	
4.	D	Tree	
5.	C	Bench	
6.	C	Tree	
7.	A	House	
8.	D	Bench	

most important aims is to turn a human being from a passive recipient and reproducer of information to a creator of new information. The student who creates information is very different from the one who is entirely oriented to copying data and passively reconstructing units of information.

This subgoal is perhaps the most important for the disadvantaged learner. In many cases, the functioning and learning deficiencies of the disadvantaged derive from their perception of themselves as passive recipients of information, and in the best case as reproducers of the information they have received. They have no expectation or even readiness to see themselves in the role of creators of information.

Many programs designed to develop problem-solving ability are based on the premise whereby the learner is made capable of problem-solving behavior. However, people with a low level of functioning lack this basic inclination. Therefore, when confronted with tasks that require the activation of new ways of thinking and new strategies, the experience of coping successfully with the challenge of these tasks leads to a change in self-perception— as someone who is able to generalize and create new information.

Pupils with a low level of functioning frequently ascribe their failure to a general lack of exposure—"I have never learned that . . . nobody taught me that . . . nobody told me to learn that . . . "—as if all their knowledge is dependent entirely on sources external to them. Dependence on outside direction was described by Zigler and Butterfield (1986) as a phenomenon typical of mentally challenged individuals. They show how this phenomenon influences the output phase, even when the problem has been satisfactorily processed, because pupils with learning difficulties do not venture to think that they are capable of resolving a problem that they have never been told how to solve. In programs designed for pupils with learning difficulties we must create, therefore, situations and conditions that will mediate the ability to generalize, to create information, and to be a more efficient learner.

THE DILEMMA BETWEEN CONTENT AND PROCESS

The process of imparting ways of thinking by means of FIE occurs, as we have said, against the background of actions that have little direct connection with the school curriculum. The instruments we have created do not teach reading, mathematics, or geography, for example, but they provide the learner with the equipment necessary to learn these subjects with greater efficiency.

Can thinking strategies be developed outside a given area of learning? Do learning strategies that do not have a specific and direct relationship to academic content areas have significance? There are those who maintain that there is no universal thinking that fits any situation and any world of content. According to this argument, instead of teaching thinking through mathematics, we must impart thinking principles in mathematics, for example, so that we shall be able to use them to solve mathematical problems.

FIE is based on an opposing view: that content is better acquired when the learner is equipped with general learning strategies and concepts that can be applied to a variety of specific learning contents. Our experience in applying FIE over the past 50 years demonstrates the efficacy of this approach.

EVIDENCE FOR THE
STRUCTURAL MODIFICATION OF THE COGNITIVE SYSTEM

FIE is capable of structurally modifying a human being's cognitive system. Over the more than 5 decades of its development and application, it has been thoroughly researched. We present one example of research that was conducted that illustrates the cognitive modification that FIE produces.

We compared two groups of pupils ages 12 to 14 who had received the FIE program with two control groups who had not received the program. The program was transmitted to one group in a boarding school context and to the second group in an external youth center context. The pupils had testable IQs ranging from 50–80 and learning performance levels of children ages 9–10. Thus, there was a gap of 3 to 4 years of learning between the learning standard and their age.

The pupils in the two trial groups received 200 hours of the FIE program over a period of 2 years, with the aim of increasing their learning ability and their modifiability. During those 2 years, the pupils in the two control groups received 200 hours of reading, writing, and mathematics learning in addition to their normal instructional exposure and in place of the additional hours of the FIE program that the trial groups received.

When we examined the children 1 year later, we found certain small but significant differences in favor of the trial groups. However, after 2 years the differences had become very pronounced. The most interesting finding was that the children who received the additional 200 of general academic enrichment did not have greater achievements than those who had not received them, despite the fact that they were at a very low level in these subjects. On the other hand, the children in the trial groups were superior to those in the control groups in everything having to do with their ways of thinking, their ability to learn, and the way in which they activated their thinking when faced with a problem. Figure 11.8 illustrates the findings of the initial study. In the graph, the solid bold line represents the control group, the solid straight line represents the normal trend line, and the broken line represents the trial groups.

Despite the fact that these differences were consistent with our expectations and predictions, we were not satisfied with them, and wished to see what would happen 3 years after the program ended. Our question was whether the differences that were found in favor of the trial groups would be maintained or would gradually disappear with time (which is typical in intervention studies of this sort). This is often referred to as *regression to the mean.*

Figure 11.8. The "Divergent Effect" Diagram

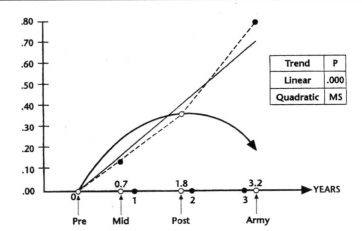

Thanks to the Israel Defense Forces, we were able to compare the results of the tests of those pupils near to their recruitment to military service. (The findings of the follow-up research are reported in Rand, Minsker, Miller, & Hoffman, 1981.) We were pleased to discover that the differences between those who had received a regular learning program and those who received the enrichment program had not disappeared but become even greater. In some of the cases, the differences had doubled or tripled in relation to the differences that had been found 3 years previously, immediately upon completing the training. The follow-up research showed an increase in the effectiveness of FIE 3 years after the termination of the treatment experience—comparing students who had FIE during their secondary school and upon entrance to the Army.

The findings testify to a structural change that took place in the population who received the program. They acquired a set of learning strategies and operational concepts, and as they gained more experience they were able to use them and to derive benefit from them, and this benefit grew increasingly with time. This can be interpreted as follows: the mental structures responsible for the learning processes are those that were modified, and this modifying process also continued beyond the time they were exposed to the program. Not only did the passage of time not weaken the instruments and the abilities that had been acquired, but it had even reinforced them the more a person utilized them in day-to-day experiences (which is an important instructional element in the teaching of the program).

Another example of research on the application and effects of the FIE program is that which has recently been reported on the FIE–Basic, the program for younger children.

THE NEED FOR ADAPTABILITY: THE RATIONALE FOR INTERVENTION AND IMPLICATIONS FOR EDUCATIONAL PROGRAMS

The discussion to this point implies the necessity for meaningful interventions that has major implications for educational programs. FIE improves the learner's adaptability to the many and swift changes that are encountered in learning situations and in life. More and more people today need enrichment, because the demand for modifiability is increasing to such an extent that even the gifted and talented need it—not because of learning deficiencies but to bring flexibility to their thinking processes and the ability to change in response to ever-increasing requirements.

The significance of this constant change from the point of view of the school, for pupils and the teachers, is that more and more information accumulates and is renewed at a rapid rate and must be conveyed and registered. The rapid rate of change, and the ever-increasing quantities of information require a change of focus with regard to the role of the school—from a focus on imparting specific factual knowledge to a focus on acquiring a learning ability that will enable the pupil to absorb and register the content of the experience. As certain facts are acquired within content disciplines, using that content in flexible, innovative, and generalized ways, and continuing to learn independently throughout one's lifetime—from school to work, and beyond—becomes absolutely vital. FIE enables us to impart to a person the ability to adapt to new situations and to solve—through the instruments—problems that are encountered for the first time.

THE RELATIONSHIP BETWEEN ASSESSMENT AND INTERVENTION

The LPAD and FIE are based on identical principles. They are very similar to one another because they have a common theoretical basis. But there is one essential difference between them. In the assessment situation the great investment in mediation is aimed to create samples of change, which serve as proof of the modifiability of the learner and enable us to take stock of the nature of the change. In the enrichment program we are dealing with the change itself. That is to say, whoever has been assessed by the LPAD and, for various reasons, found to require a special intervention to increase modifiability and adaptability, will be able to receive this through Instrumental Enrichment. Put another way, the goal of the LPAD is not to teach to mastery, but to identify areas and functions where mastery is either possible or a worthy goal to pursue.

The relationship between assessment (LPAD) and intervention (FIE) can be clarified if we return to our basic formulation the transformation required in the three partners in the learning process—the teacher, the pupil, and the subject matter:

1. For example, as a rule pupils are not prepared to think about materials learned in history and to retrieve from them the general concepts, principles, and thinking process contained in them. Therefore, what is needed is the ability to use strategic skills to move to this level of interaction with content and the presence of a reframed curriculum that makes this possible—transformations in two of the partners, the students and the curriculum.
2. Teachers often find it difficult to combine the regular syllabus with thinking processes. Teachers must learn to deal with *thinking* as a content world in itself. One has to know, for example, how to stop in the middle of a literature lesson and say: "Now we shall make an analysis of symbols and different thinking operations." Furthermore, to enable pupils to acquire thinking processes, teachers must expose them to performing tasks based on these processes. However, teachers—as a consequence of their training and the curriculum demands of the school—are often unable to create such a syllabus and seldom have the time and interest to pursue it. Thus we must consider two other types of transformations—the teacher must be trained and encouraged to use approaches based on the retrieval of thinking processes from within the content world of the typical curriculum—thus changing the curriculum and the teacher.
3. The last issue arises from the substance of the academic discipline—that is, from the content world itself. From this perspective, the analysis of the learning process in the course of learning a subject limits the content of the learning process, which has its own continuity and learning principles. The subject matter requires a certain progression—moving from the easy to the difficult, from the known to the unknown—according to principles arising out of the content. We hold to entirely different principles in the use of content to develop the ability to learn. Bridging by means of the teacher/mediator and the pupils themselves—taking the learned principles acquired in the FIE program and transferring them, with the teacher's help, to the subject(s) being studied—will further the process of cognition. If students have learned to be systematic, they will work systematically also when they are learning history. If they have learned to be exact and to use more than one source of information, they will transfer these abilities in order to resolve problems in mathematics. To this end, the teacher must give pupils an insight into the essence of the subject to which the bridge leads and instruct them how not to think about the unit of acquired knowledge as a solitary unit but as a bridge linking it with the different study subjects and every area of life—yet another important transformation.

FIE, precisely because it is not based on any specific content world, represents a source for transference from one area to another and makes it possible to turn a human being into a more active and efficient learner.

CHAPTER 12

Preparation and Prevention Through Early Intervention: The Feuerstein Instrumental Enrichment–Basic (FIE-B) Program

Early intervention holds the promise of prevention. That should be our ultimate goal! In today's world, the chance that children will be considered to have a learning disability (LD) is very high—some educators point out that the rate of children diagnosed with a LD can be as high as 25%. Could we be witnessing a modern epidemic? There have been many definitions and reasons advanced for the incidence of the failure to learn, but the research has not been able to definitively pinpoint the causes. From our point of view, there is a much more important question: Can learning disabilities be prevented, or at the very least can the risk be reduced? Our answer has been addressed in earlier chapters of this book, and in this chapter we take the response further. Here we propose the concept and strategy of prevention that is linked to early and systematic intervention.

Rather than categorizing a learning difficulty as an inherent problem with the child's thinking skills, we see it as a consequence of a lack of appropriate mediation of the particular cognitive functions that cause difficulties in learning. For example, a child who behaves impulsively could have trouble reading because he or she is identifying whole words on the basis of one or more familiar syllables, reading "egg" for "leg," for instance. Such a child may experience blurred and sweeping perception. Alternatively, a child whose orientation in space is insufficiently developed will skip letters. A child who has trouble with precision at the input stage will decode the word correctly but produce incorrect sounds, not because the child does not know how to produce correct sounds but because there is a lack of the necessary precision or the appropriate strategies to be precise. In some cases, children described as dyslexic have trouble decoding symbols and seeing the connection between them and reality. These examples reflect the use of cognitive functions to understand and ultimately prevent or limit learning disability through intervention (see Chapter 9).

From our perspective, learning disabilities are closely related to the development of the cognitive functions. Thus, radically changing the way the deficiency is both defined and dealt with allows us the potential to remedy LD through mediation and rehabilitate the student. LDs are not rigid or fixed traits, but states that can be changed. For the young child— the "developing" learner—the promising potential is in preparation and prevention.

OVERVIEW OF THE
FEUERSTEIN INSTRUMENTAL ENRICHMENT-BASIC (FIE–B) PROGRAM

The fundamental premise underlying the FIE–B program is that human development is dependent on a critical mass of mediation given to the child by his/her parents and environment. In order for the child to be able to develop critical skills such as language, social knowledge, and the symbol systems of the culture (i.e., the academic skills—reading, spelling, arithmetic, writing, behavior, etc.), he or she must be equipped with learning and thinking skills. These are the necessary foundation for later learning. The child needs to receive mediation for focusing, comparison, precision, behavior control, and other mental operations in order to benefit from institutionalized learning procedures or from informal learning procedures (i.e., family, neighbors, social relationships). This depends on the existence of preliminary learning conditions (i.e., cognitive functions leading to mental operations, as we have described them earlier in this book).

In our view, many of the children labeled "learning disabled" actually suffer from a lack of mediation. For this reason, the primary goal of the FIE–B program is to equip young children with learning and thinking skills essential for future learning and in this way diminish the growing epidemic of learning deficiencies. Our point of view on this issue can be summarized as: "Don't say learning deficiency; say rather teaching deficiency." We put this into practice by carefully training teachers and parents in order to (1) equip them with a powerful cognitive tool that will help them to prepare their pupils for the later learning that they will encounter, and (2) turn them into mediators--not just with the FIE–B instruments but also by creating a repertoire of mediational strategies that can be applied to the many life events that present a platform for mediation.

A DESCRIPTION OF THE INSTRUMENTS

The instruments of the FIE–B are organized into the following groups, according to their contribution to cognitive development:

Instruments That Focus on Perceptual/Motor Development:

- *Organization of Dots (Basic).* Drawing lines to connect dots that create order and meaning from information that is initially perceived as disconnected and scattered.
- *Tri-Channel Attentional Learning.* Exploring shapes using fingers but not seeing (tactile), and then identifying them through drawing (graphic) and differentiating them from other similar shapes (visual).

Instruments That Focus on Spatial Orientation, Oriented Toward Verbal Labeling:

- *Orientation in Space (Basic).* Learning to use a vocabulary to orient and describe objects in space—such as top/bottom, in front of/in back of, inside/outside, etc.

Instruments That Focus on Social/Emotional Awareness:

- *Identifying Emotions.* Identifying emotional expressions and applying the emotions to appropriate social situations.
- *From Empathy to Awareness.* Deciphering emotional conditions in problem situations and identifying appropriate resolutions of the problem or conflict.
- *Think and Learn to Prevent Violence.* Identification of conflict situations and considering the outcomes of alternative ways of responding.

Instruments That Focus on Abstract and Integrative Thinking:

- *From Unit to Group.* Establishing concepts of units, groups of units, and number of units. Leading to clarification of number concepts and summative behavior.
- *Compare and Discover the Absurd (Levels I and II).* Using comparative criteria to identify and differentiate situations that present incongruity. Level II tasks involve categorization, differentiation, and insightful analysis.
- *Learning to Ask Questions for Reading Comprehension.* Using pictorial and verbal information to answer questions and formulate sentences and thematic meaning based on the "stories" provided through different types and levels of information.

Instruments That Focus on Content Knowledge:

- *Know and Identify.* Labels and identifies functions of commonly known objects, adding classification, inference, and functional differentiations.

Each instrument uses a variety of ways of presenting information, and provides opportunities, through the structure of the material and the manner of mediation to develop concepts and modalities of thinking. There are many aspects of the program that must be incorporated for it to effectively reach its goals. These are acquired in the training, and are conveyed in the supporting materials for the program (the instruments themselves and the User's Guide) that are provided for the teacher or parent who receives training.

RESPONDING TO THE
YOUNG CHILD AND TO SPECIAL NEEDS CHILDREN

Differentiating FIE–B from FIE-Standard

The standard Instrumental Enrichment (FIE-S) program (see Chapter 11) requires a level of necessary proficiency that makes it difficult for special education therapists and teachers to use it with particularly low-functioning groups. For this reason, the FIE instruments were adapted so that they can be used with these groups. For both regular and special needs populations, the adaptation focused on the following changes: lower levels of abstraction and complexity (i.e., the amount of information is relatively lower and the level of familiarity higher) and increased and more prominent use of colorful and engaging "cartoon-like" drawings that reflect the world of children and capture their interest. It should be noted that the level of abstraction and the level of perception required, as well as the level of complexity, are still relatively high and challenging for children, so the instruments are by no means "easy"—quite the contrary. However, the instruments are presented in such a way as to make them attractive to children and their therapists and teachers.

There are two areas where the FIE–B battery makes fundamental changes from the FIE-S:

The instruments present more demands for the mastery of content. FIE-S is more focused processes of fluid intelligence (i.e., generalized and abstractive principles of thinking), while the FIE–B focuses more on crystal components of intelligence (i.e., the concrete content of experience). There are several reasons for this. First, the separation between the intelligences does not exist at young ages or at low levels of functioning, so more exposure to specific content is needed, and second, the developing child as well as the special needs child is presumed to need wide and repeated exposure to general knowledge in order to assure their correct development. Lastly, due to the level of transfer in the initial stages, the instruments' concrete examples allow for easier transfer to reality.

FIE–B also addresses the emotional-behavioral dimension through the inclusion of three tools that address social/emotional learning situations. Our view that this is an important element of early learning experience with important implications for later cognitive development, and that it is an implicit foundation for much of the symbolic and abstractive learning that is required for development. Another important reason for including the social/emotional dimension is that it allows the creation of better socialization mechanisms in young children, which prepares them for integration in school society. To special needs children it is necessary for them to be integrated into normative society. A child who is unable to identify his own classmate's emotions (for an example, see Figure 12.1) will not be able to opt for the correct action to realize the appropriate emotion and will be unable to solve a conflict. Such children will find it very difficult to fit and even to survive in regular society.

Figure 12.1. FIE–B "Identifying Emotions" Activity

Responding to the Autistic Child: A Case in Point

Another reason for the inclusion of the emotional theme in the FIE–B battery was our wish to offer children within the autistic spectrum and others with similar difficulties in social development an opportunity to be exposed to social/emotional learning. Diverse theories link the problems of autistic children to the fact that they find it difficult to decipher other people's emotions and thoughts. A prominent scholar (Baron-Cohen, 1995) has stated that teaching children with autistic features how to comprehend human emotions is particularly important, taking into account a popular theory that these children lack a "theory of mind." The instruments that focus on emotions (see Figure 12.2) teach the child how to decipher the facial and body language of other people and how to establish the relation between their facial expressions and incidents happening in the surrounding. These are important aspects of social awareness and social cognition for many children.

Figure 12.2. FIE–B "From Empathy to Action" Activity

Using FIE-B in Therapy

The FIE–B battery of instruments puts powerful tools in the hands of not just teachers and parents but also therapists—including occupational and speech therapists and, of course, psychologists. The FIE–B battery gives therapists three additional channels of treatment:

Therapists open up an additional interventional channel, enabling the reinforcement of learning and thinking skills by addressing relevant content (in the therapeutic contexts) and by adding mediated learning experience modalities to their repertoire.

Therapists can use treatment situations, consistent with their particular goals, but turn them into meditational situations. Suppose an occupational therapist is working on the pencil grip of a young Down syndrome child. The FIE–B Orientation in Space instrument can be used to teach the child the spatial concepts relevant to pencil grip (right hand, pencil point down and eraser up, the three fingers that grip the pencil hold the bottom of the pencil, etc.). A speech therapist attempting to make a child use concepts could use the Compare and Discover the Absurd (see Figure 12.3) to develop comparison skills that enhance the value of learning aids used in the treatment situation.

Figure 12.3. FIE–B "Compare and Discover the Absurd"Activity

***The therapist has the opportunity to mediate and to teach the prereq-
uisite conditions for success to the subject.*** Let us suppose that the child
has a poor emotional vocabulary and a poor understanding of others. The
therapist can create a platform of concepts to facilitate treatment. A great
many therapists use behaviorist approaches that we feel may be limited,
as they do not activate the cognitive channel in the child. Occupational
therapists will find that their life is easier if they can involve the subject's
cognition in his work on motor skills. For example, instead of simply using
contact or imitation to accompany instruction, instruction can be given
using the appropriate muscles while at the same time using correct planning and decision-making. However, doing this requires those prerequisites
that will enable the production of what can be called "top-down" strategies,
from concept to action. This essential preparation can be found in the FIE–B
Organization of Dots instrument (see Figure 12.4), where the subject creates a connection between the cognitive dimension and the visual-motor
dimension. With the FIE–B instruments Orientation in Space and From Unit
to Group, the therapist can help the subject to improve the ability to obey
increasingly complex instructions while keeping in mind the content of the
instruction even when the task is ongoing or replete with distractions.

The cognitive-dynamic approach aims at setting the changes produced
by the different therapists on a sort of schema of cognitive action. In this
way, as an example, the ability of the child functioning within the autistic
spectrum to establish eye contact with others will be based on an understanding of the essence of human relationships and the understanding of
the meaning of communication in interpersonal relations. From this point
of view, the meditational-cognitive element should be the major channel to
be used by therapists, and training in the instruments has the potential to
add a mediational component to a great many therapeutic situations.

Figure 12.4. FIE–B "Organization of Dots" Activity

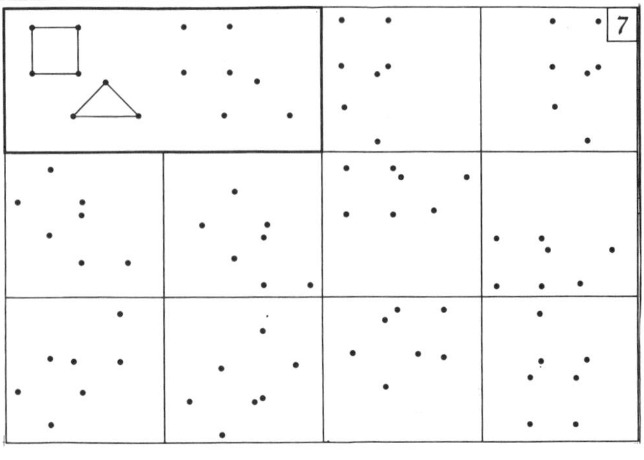

RESEARCH ON THE FIE-B PROGRAM

The FIE–B program is approximately 7 years old, which is relatively new when compared to the almost 50-year life span of the FIE-S. In those 7 years, however, many teachers and parents have been trained in its use and have applied it in classrooms, clinics, and in home teaching settings. Recently a research study was published exploring its effectiveness in 5 countries (Canada, Chile, Belgium, Italy, and Israel) with children who have a variety of special needs (ADHD, intellectual impairments of a genetic origin, autistic spectrum disorders, and other learning disabilities). The results of this comparative study indicated that cognitive functioning was improved for children with developmental disabilities, that no advantages were experienced for specific disabilities, and that greater cognitive gains occurred when children received the program in an educational context (classroom groups) where all teachers were committed (and well trained) in the principles and practices of mediated learning (Kozulin et al., 2009).

WHY ARE PREPARATION AND PREVENTION NECESSARY?

The crucial question for parents and teachers is how should we prepare our children for school? What do they need to succeed? Long years of study and high levels of functioning are ahead of them. How can we adequately prepare them? Parents are faced with multiple options and resources—toys, games, stimulation, and remediation programs. Academic curricula are getting more complex and abstract at earlier and earlier levels—in developed countries kindergartens are becoming academic learning centers. We are reminded of the kindergarten student who exclaimed with frustration: "I do not know how to read, I cannot write, and they won't let me talk. I am wasting my time here!"

What is the answer? Throughout this book we make the point that we must teach our children how to learn. We must do it at an early age, and with all of the natural and available resources available in the lives of children and their families. Some children are able to learn readily and rapidly. Others will need systematic and focused exposure to benefit from the stimulation and resources around them. The FIE–B program was designed with this in mind, and is applied to enable all children to gather data, control behavior, understand the problems confronted, and embark on courses of actions that not only responds to that which are encountered but provides a springboard to other and new experiences. There are many aspects to this development that we address throughout this book. For the young and developing child, the hoped-for outcomes are to be able to distinguish between relevant and irrelevant facts, bring up assumptions and appraise them, sum up what is learned, and create an overall integrative picture. Some of the resulting skills will involve learning how to: express and apply conclusions from a process of elaboration, compare sources of information, and understand the emotions of others and their relevance to the social experiences and interpersonal conflicts encountered in life.

These are clearly the prerequisites of any learning process and of the whole world of learning experiences awaiting the developing child. The FIE–B program appears to be a promising resource in helping the developing learner to be ready and successful!

CHAPTER 13

Shaping Supportive Environments

In Chapters 10 and 11 we have described two applied methods arising from the theory of structural cognitive modifiability (SCM) and the theory and application of mediated learning experience (MLE). The application of these methods of assessment and intervention enable human beings to be amenable to the processes of change that previously were considered to be non-existent. These two methods developed from the general belief that a human being is modifiable, but will this belief be sufficient to create the conditions for actual, manifest modifiability? Moreover, is it enough to increase individuals' learning ability and to provide them with the tools for learning for them to be modified? Will these changes, when produced, be sustained, encouraged, and elaborated upon in the future?

Our experience with the implementation of the two applied programs have convinced us that it is not enough to know about a human being's modifiability, and even increasing modifiability is not sufficient for this purpose. In order to enable or even demand a person's modification, we must design a supportive environment.

We have learned from observing different environments that there are situations that do not enable a person to be modified because everything in them is built in such a way as to cause the person to persist and remain in the same condition, confirmed by the expectations, structures, and well-meaning individuals in that environment. In such an environment, the change that has been proven possible through dynamic assessment and dynamic learning experiences are denied the person even after modifiability has been demonstrated and increased by means of our interventions. In some cases, the changes we have produced are denied, seriously denigrated, or acknowledged with the passive acceptance that little or nothing can be done about it because it is too costly, too difficult to provide, or that needed resources are not available. We counter that such postures reflect a lack of need for and belief in modifiability.

AN ENVIRONMENT THAT PREVENTS OR ACTS AGAINST CHANGE

Generally speaking, if the environment does not require the person to be modified but adapts itself to him or her—what has been called an *autoplastic response*—meaningful and sustained change will not occur. The environment of the special education classroom or school illustrates this characteristic well. These schools—their curricula and personnel—are based on very good intentions, but they create an environment that conforms to the pupil's current ability and not the ability that could likely be attained if and when pupils are called on to function at a different level. The environment of the special education school conforms itself, as it were, to the pupil's abilities, instead of setting challenges of adaptation to new and more demanding situations. Students are not required to invest an effort to adapt to challenges, and expectations for higher levels of performance are not formulated or conveyed. Thus, such placements do not utilize educative potentials to be discovered and increased.

Environments That Deny the Opportunity for Modifiability

Modification-blocking environments say to a person: "We know who you are. We know that you are unmodifiable. We do not expect you to be modified." Therefore, the environment does not equip a human being with the tools needed to adapt, nor does it provide the opportunity to become adaptable. A modification-denying environment not only fails to confront the person with challenges and situations that must be adapted to in order to survive, but also fails to provide exposure and training with tools that will enable adaptation. It also does not give the time and support needed to successfully adapt. In the absence of these elements—the suitable tools of thinking and learning, on the one hand, and the readiness to give the opportunity to work toward this adaptation, on the other—the adaptation processes are liable to be very difficult, even impossible.

The Dangers of Homogeneous Environments: Accepting Individuals as They Are

It is our contention that one of the main factors behind the blockage of the processes of change in special education environments is the homogeneous character of the children being placed there—a society of people formed according to the criteria of their limitations—because of their inability to adapt. Such a society of low achievers is thus treated with very low expectations for the ability to learn or change, and the results of such placements confirm the expectations.

In an environment that blocks (or does not promote) change, the focus is on current ability levels instead of potential abilities, and thus leaves individuals in their situations without modification. There are environments that transmit to the person the clear (and sometimes comfortable message): "remain in the place where you are, and you will be assured of a comfortable existence and a good feeling." The basic premise underlying these environments, whereby a human being is viewed as nonmodifiable, leads to a passive approach that accepts the persons as they are and does everything to prevent the appearance of tensions between current levels of functioning and the level required in a modification-encouraging environment. It is important to clearly define the components of this position.

- *The passive-acceptant approach:* This is a product of the premise according to which a person is unmodifiable, leading to the creation of environmental conditions that are in line with the person's current ability and do not stretch the person toward the abilities that he or she would be capable of developing were it demanded of them.
- *The tension between current levels of functioning and potential:* The nonmodifying environment denies a person the needed tension arising from the gap between the current functional situation and the potential for higher functioning. It is a tension because demands for change and different levels of functioning require efforts, risks, resources, and—above all—belief and commitment from helping resources (teachers, parents, and the diverse range of professional specialists).

Yet, there are those who argue that the best solution for the disabled person, whatever the nature of the disability, will be to provide an environment where he or she will not be called upon to do more than is possible in the current situation. This point of view is vividly illustrated by the case of a 24-year-old male Down syndrome patient who was brought to me for assessment. The boy's father asked, "Please, do me a favor. Don't teach him things that he doesn't know." The request was made as an expression of his concern lest too great a tension was caused in his son. "If so," the father was asked, "why do you bring him to us? What he knows we do not need to teach, whereas what he doesn't know you would not allow us to teach him?" The young man was brought into the room and he knew how to read and was even working as a librarian, but he did not know which was the right side of the person standing in front of him, and in certain tests he was unable to function. Within a very short space of time he was taught to function. Whatever tension the father felt was easily dissipated when we began to work with him.

Thus, the tendency to accept a person passively is the result of an assumption about the inability of modifying the situation. Our approach, on the other hand, is an active, modifying approach, based on the belief in the possibilities of modification.

THE SHAPING OF MODIFYING ENVIRONMENTS

The key question, therefore, is how to create an environmental engineering (similar to human engineering) that can serve as a basis for designing environments that will encourage, reinforce, and create in the student the will, the need, and the ability to be modified.

It is this need, and the positive answers to the questions we have posed in this book and in our work, that leads us to the development of strategies and programs to create environments that encourage and facilitate conditions that support the modifiability of human functioning and student development. Ironically, it has been called by some a new paradigm. It is new only in the recognition that change is possible, and, if so, structures and training, resources and commitments must be devoted to making these changes possible. We thus need to work with decision makers and program implementers to bring into reality those conditions (rules, curricula, training, consultation, and resource support) that foster human modifiability. Such actions range across a diversity of populations and applications.

The creation of these conditions requires that the theory of SCM and MLE be understood and practiced. To this end, awareness and familiarity with the theory and its application are required. Specific training for parents, childcare providers, professional specialists, and others can facilitate the planning and conducting of programs that infuse a human modifiability perspective into interventions and the institutional programs that support them. Sometimes whole new programs need to be developed. In other instances, existing programs can be modified to meet the goals and needs of this new paradigm.

Program Identification and Development

Within the context of SCM and MLE, we can work with concerned decision-makers and planners to help design interventions that will create the potential for modifiability. Needs assessments, reviews of potential interventions, and demonstrations of how such interventions can facilitate change are options to materialize these potentials. Mobilization of resources and involvement of key personnel are important strategies to make programs viable and appealing. This requires sensitive and ongoing consultation and the marshalling of conceptual and material resources, often sharing successful interventions of others and then tailoring program dimensions of relevance to the targeted environment. The critical elements in this approach are a careful and accurate analysis of the system dimensions that must be reflected in planning and an offering of encouragement and support to develop specific operational plans.

Examples of such sharing can be cited in large-scale programs in the State of Bahia in Brazil and the Taunton School District (near Boston in the United States), or in smaller-scale applications such as the Mediated Learning Academy in Vancouver, British Colombia. These programs can be used as models of the applications and attributes of program development—to demonstrate that it is indeed possible to create conditions for systemic and meaningful modifiability.

Examples of systemic awareness in schools are: paying attention to such variables as classroom organization, placing students into classes where FIE is offered, enabling teachers to observe and support one another in the application of the program, and providing for group support meetings with ongoing training and peer consultation. All of these elements require strategic planning, monitoring, and making ongoing adaptations in light of circumstances and the changing contexts presented by environments.

Training in the Application of MLE

The providers of MLE such as teachers, parents, childcare workers, and therapeutic support personnel (such as psychologists, social workers, speech and language therapists, occupational and physical therapists, etc.) can be trained to identify appropriate applications of mediation and apply them to meet the needs of students, children, and clients. Several very innovative curricula for such training have been developed and applied in a number of countries globally and in diverse settings and populations.

Consultation and Follow Up

Sustaining, supporting, and further developing programs that shape modifying environments requires periodic and ongoing consultation. Dynamic assessment results are not frozen in time. As the learner changes, re-evaluation is needed and valuable, and results and implications must be shared with teachers and parents. The development and adjustment of recommendations also require ongoing contacts. Written reports and the conveyance of information, combined with planning activities, also contribute to the process of focusing on modifiability potential.

SUMMARIZING THE ISSUES

Our experience has been that when such efforts are undertaken many changes are possible, and both attitudes and actions need to be taken that go well beyond the specific application of the LPAD and FIE. The environment in which these applications are developed and provided requires a third element—being shaped in a way that makes these changes possible. However powerful and successful the LPAD and FIE are, they are not enough in and of themselves. Perhaps the most vivid confirmation of this is the many teachers and parents who have told us (and whom we have observed) that once they have learned FIE and MLE (and adopted the belief and expectation of human modifiability) their whole perspective and range of functioning has been changed. Parents describe how their interactions with their children are different when they apply principles of MLE to their day-to-day family interactions. Teachers tell us how they are teaching their subject matter areas from very different—and more satisfying—perspectives. But, unfortunately, we also hear these same teachers and parents describing how often the structures of the schools, day care centers, and responses of the support personnel (administrators, therapy providers, medical and social providers) do not encourage or at times even reject the changes that have been experienced.

The clear message must be that these new perspectives, skills, and awarenesses need a welcoming, engaging, and facilitating environment to make them happen and to sustain them over time and in the face of pressures to reduce or abandon commitments. Our experience with over 50 years of implementation, and much research, has convinced us of this need.

Thus, shaping a modifying environment requires an active, continuous, and multifaceted development and application of strategies for affecting environmental awareness and commitment to the goals and potentials of cognitive modifiability.

The applied methods arising from SCM and MLE cannot be implemented successfully in practice or even be able to exist unless there exists the first condition—namely, the belief that a human being can be modified. Here we intentionally return to our emphasis on the need for a belief that is generated by a commitment to the modifiability of human beings (the need)—the belief is an expression of our responsibility to those who need our help, and can benefit, to modify themselves and adapt. In the wake of the belief, we then create the means, the methodology, and the research that gives our belief a scientific basis. But belief is the primary condition. Many wonderful methods have failed because belief was lacking in them, which led to an absence of commitment.

The applied methods and the tools derived from them are crucial, as is the need to interact in the environment in ways that support modifiability. The demonstration of ongoing commitment and persistent activities, and the bringing of new resources to materialize this commitment (such as the LPAD and FIE), will contribute to shaping the environment according to this perspective.

In the final chapter of this book we offer newly developing support for this point of view and link our theory and concepts to the great revolution in the brain sciences, as well as to our experience with implementation of the programs and theory that we have described. With such convincing support, perhaps it will not be so difficult to create the condition for cognitive modifiability in our environments.

CHAPTER 14

New Neuroscience Findings on the Brain/Mind's Capacity for Change: An Epilogue

During the more than 60 years that has encompassed the development of the theory of structural cognitive modifiability (SCM) and the application of mediated learning experience (MLE), we limited ourselves to defining modifiability as occurring primarily within the realm of behavior. Yet, we speculated quietly and privately that these changes must have a neurophysiological correlate. We discussed our theories and speculations with many of the preeminent neurologists and scholars of the time, but none of us dared to state equivocally that such was the case. The technology of the time just did not permit further study, and we feared that we would be considered wild dreamers without a scientific foundation. And yet we knew that there had to be a connection, and that the observed behavior must have been generated by concomitant changes in the neural system.

Even our theory of SCM, referring to changes in the mental behavior of the individual, was subject to a struggle with those who considered human behavior from a fixist position—reflected in static measurement procedures such as IQ tests (such as Binet-Simon, Terman, Wechsler, and so forth) and other manifestations in theory and practice.

Nonetheless, never in the senior author's most daring propositions would he have proposed that the changes observed following interventions were concomitant to, or the result of, changes in the neural system. It was hoped that this would be the case, and it was thought that it would be impossible to fully explain the changes without such a relationship, but we concluded that we could not speculate beyond our immediate observations. You could not affect chromosomes, irrespective of how much learning occurred; you could not affect the genes. This was part of the old nature-versus-nurture dilemma. There were those who claimed (and still do—see, for example, Herrnstein and Murray, 1994) that 85% of the variance in measurable intelligence is due to nature (one's genetic inheritance) and only 15% due to nurture (the environmental factors). This position holds that there is a limited amount of potential for change, comprising approximately one standard deviation, with the remainder of functional potential being constant.

REVISING THE "SCIENCE" OF THE BRAIN

Today, however, the neurosciences bring us evidence not only of the modifiability of the individual's mental functions, but also that the changes that can be produced are in some ways (although not yet totally defined) not merely behavioral manifestations. They are not just changes in the structure of the behavior, of the mental processes, but are actually related to changes in both the hardware and the software of the neural system. It is now no exaggeration to state that *the neural system is modified by the behavior, no less than the behavior is determined by the neural system.*

This is now a time of tremendous change in the methodology and focus on the science of brain studies which has been, to a large extent, made possible by the noninvasive technologies. This affords us an almost daily expansion and revision of our concepts and understandings. A review of the research today will be limited and to some degree obsolete tomorrow simply because of the sheer volume of studies and discoveries that seem to come almost daily. New possibilities are being considered, existent ideas regarding structures and functions are being questioned and reframed, and innovative approaches to studying the brain are emerging that reflect tremendous creative energy and an openness to the richness of the variables under consideration.

NEUROPLASTICITY: ULTIMATE SUPPORT FOR THE THEORY OF STRUCTURAL COGNITIVE MODIFIABILITY

The enormous amount of work done on the changes produced in the brain encourages us to ask two major questions: (1) What is the nature of the changes? and (2) What are the kinds of environmental conditions that may produce the changes?

Here we must take the reader into a more technical discourse than has been provided in this book up to this point. It is necessary to fully understand the meaning of the new research, and how it confirms and supports the cognitive modifiability in its theoretical and practical aspects.

We are now much better able to explain SCM and MLE by relating them to recent advances in understanding the neurophysiology of brain responses, particularly the discovery of the existence of the *mirror neurons* and their contribution to neuroplasticity. It is now possible to actively view the effects of SCM and the provision of MLE on the development and modification of neurophysiological processes. The noninvasive neurological research methodologies (MRI, fMRI, CAT, PET, TMS, etc.) make possible a great deal of direct observation in real time and foster an understanding of the neuro-physical foundations for cognitive modifiability.

From these perspectives, we can extend our concepts of SCM and MLE beyond the developmental and experiential perspective, confirming that the provision of MLE to modify learning and behavioral functions has a very sound neurological basis. We can now confidently speculate, pending further confirmation that MLE appears to act on the mirror neurons, creating changes not only in the observable behavior but also in neurological structure and activity. These mechanisms within the brain exist and are distributed more widely throughout the cortex than initially thought. Although our knowledge about these mechanisms is still in an early and not fully differentiated stage, there is evidence that they are activated by observations of actions that are imitated and then structurally integrated. In our work on language stimulation and development (Feuerstein & Falik, in press), we described a process we call "mediated soliloquy—MSL," we propose that the mirror neurons are triggered in the child's brain upon hearing language, *as if* the child were using these structures him- or herself.

This elevates the process of *imitative learning* to a very prominent position. The language area in the brain is particularly rich in these mirror neurons. In fact, it is now known that Broca's area in the brain is responsible for more than language functions and extends to a variety of motor and sensory functions (further explaining the neurophysiological correlates to the neuronal mirroring that we now understand to be central to MSL phenomena). In fact, the whole concept of localization of functions is undergoing serious challenge (see Doidge, 2007).

There is now considerable scientific speculation (reflected in the work of researchers like Skoyles, 2008) that the imitative process is linked to motor aspects of speech and a variety of other behaviors. As an example, when a child is exposed to phonetic input, articulatory processes are initiated. The brain then makes neurological connections that lead to the mimicking of speech sounds (as described by Liberman and Mattingly, 1989). Skoyles offers a number of hypotheses based on the new neurophysiological evidence that imitation in language development goes well beyond or, in our words, *deeply into* the brain. He summarizes that "imitation, in spite of playing a mostly transient role in language acquisition, is a necessary process for the existence of speech" (p. 3). Some interesting elaborations of this speculation are offered by Skoyles as he reviews the research in this area. He summarizes his theoretical position regarding the motor and neurological basis for the role of imitation (in relation to the phenomenon of mirror neurons) as follows: "speech will arise both evolutionally and developmentally *around motor imitation circuits in cooperation with those brain areas processing auditory invariants* (and) the processes behind speech will be amodal enabling non-auditory based forms of language" (p. 9; emphasis added).

We believe that this model extends well beyond the area of speech and language development to the diverse range of experience in the world, consolidating imitative activity and elaborating it both *internally* (thinking and understanding) and *externally* (into linguistic and motor behavior). These conclusions receive further elaboration and validation by the work of Fogassi and Ferrari (2007) who summarize several important studies describing the effect of exposure to certain verbal stimuli, and to the gestures and meanings that accompany them, leading to such linguistic functions as enhancing the tongue and muscle activities, with implications well beyond. On a behavioral level this correlates to activity in the brain, whereby the mirror neurons play a meaningful role in articulated language expression and neurophysiological activity. Rizzolatti and Craighero (2004) demonstrate that when an object is seen, its visual features activate the motor knowledge necessary to interact with it. We draw the implication that when meaningful experience is processed by the brain, the mirror neurons are activated to support and elaborate the imitative process. Daniel Goleman, in his book *Social Intelligence* (2006), reviews the developing research describing mirror neurons as "reflecting back an action we observe in someone else, making us mimic that action or have the impulse to do so" (p. 41).

Other aspects of a focus on language development that support the dynamics of SCM and MLE are those studies that link meaning (in language and speech production) to performance and show enhanced congruence between observation (of behavior) and motor responses. We believe that this strengthens the linkage—between the language, motor, and ultimately neurophysiological patterning—generated by the activities that we structure in MLE, and makes it both a complex and powerful experience.

In areas such as gestural communication (Rizzolatti & Arbib, 1998), the evolution of speech (cf., Mesiter et al., 2003; Seyal et al., 1999), and auditory sensitivity (Kohler et al., 2002), the effects of various external stimulation and experiences on neurophysiological processes have been observed. We consider the research on these functions to be still somewhat microcosmic—that is, focusing on small aspects of larger integrated functions. But it is suggestive and highly encouraging.

The mirror neurons help us better understand the processes of neural restructuring that we propose occurs in SCM and MLE. Scientists are now convinced (see Rizzolatti & Craighero, 2004) that "each time an individual sees an action done by another individual, neurons that represent that action are activated in the observer's premotor cortex . . . thus, the mirror system transforms visual information into knowledge" (p. 172). We suggest that this occurs in other areas of the brain as well.

The researchers' goals have been to design studies where the mental representation of an action triggers the activity of the mirror neurons, which then leads to elaborated sensory or motor actions (that can be related back to initial causation). In an ingenious and very interesting study designed by Umilta and colleagues (2002), monkeys who observed activities in which they "understood" the action (e.g., placing food to be eaten behind a screen) experienced a discharge of mirror neurons even though they did not observe the final outcome of the action. When an action was simply mimed—that is, not presented realistically—the mirror neurons were not activated. From our point of view, this can be explained in MLE terms. The placing of the food within the monkey's view was an intentional act. Concealing it caused a representational process to be initiated, leading to neurological responses corresponding to transcendence and meaning. The monkeys were "thinking" about the situation, and activating neurological mechanisms as though they were experiencing it—which in fact they were!

Rizzolatti and Craighero, in reviewing mirror neuron research on human subjects, indicate that TMS studies indicate "that a mirror neuron system . . . exists in humans and that it possesses important properties not observed in monkeys" (p. 176). Interestingly, humans appear to activate mirror neurons for movements forming (or leading to) an action and do not need to observe the fully manifested action (as do the monkeys). Again, this provides suggestive evidence for the role of the mirror neurons in the higher cognitive functions (using generalization processes and the functions of symbols). Other researchers (cf., Schubotz & Von Cramon, 2001, 2002 a, b) conclude that the mirror neuron system plays a role in such mental operations as the representation of sequential information that is experienced to varying degrees of direct visual and motor exposure.

An important implication of this work is the linkages between action (the doing) and communication (the language) provide what Rizzolatti and Arbib (1998) describe as the link between actor and observer, the sender and receiver of the message. This is central to our understanding of the mechanisms that enable MLE to materialize SCM and offer convincing support for both the theory and the functional linkages.

THE ROLE OF MIRROR NEURONS IN COGNITIVE DEVELOPMENT

The conclusions that can be drawn from the research on mirror neurons confirm a direct relationship between the active behavioral interventions of MLE and cognitive development and modifiability. The relationship is reciprocal and supportive—each contributes to the other. When we provide behavioral models for the developing learner, we activate neural circuits in the brain that in turn further activate other cortical functions. From a functional point of view, there is now clear evidence that this mechanism is enhanced by repetitive actions that stimulate imitative learning (Iacoboni et al., 1999; Buccino et al., 2004)—confirming the role of repetition with variations that is central in our application of MLE.

The great puzzle of imitative behavior when we consider it in relation to language development is how it permits acquisition of many areas of activities that occur outside our direct awareness. We now think that the role of the mirror neurons is a potential answer, and it permits great optimism regarding the more general process of creating structural cognitive (and neurophysical) modifiability. As we learn more with the coming research advances, we are hopeful that this mechanism in the brain will help us to further understand how observed (and imitated) phenomena can have the same effect on the neuron as the acted-out behavior. As shown in the area of language acquisition, even the sound related to a certain unobserved behavior has the same effects as the observed act. This has major implications for further understanding of the mechanisms put into effect through the provision of MLE.

For example, when we describe the MLE parameter of intentionality/reciprocity (see Chapter 6), we can now understand the process in clear neurophysiological terms. The brain *sees* what the actor (the mediator) is doing, and then *understands* why the actor is doing it. It is now becoming clear that this occurs in a very integral way, processed in the neural system. It can thus be concluded that the intention of the actions can be conveyed, processed, and the mechanism is the selective activation of the mirror neuron system. The new research is showing (cf., Iacoboni et al., 2005) that what is mirrored is not only the meaning of the actions (observed) but also the understanding of other's intentions.

This extends very broadly, moving from areas such as language acquisition to the mediation of empathy and emotional understanding. It has been demonstrated by ingenious studies where human subjects were exposed to pleasant and painful stimuli, related to facial expressions of others, and experienced activation of their neural systems in relevant and consistent ways (Carr et al., 2003; Saarela et al., 2007; Singer, 2006; Wicker et al., 2003). Other researchers (see Gallese et al., 2004) summarize these experiments by suggesting that feeling emotions is due to the activation of circuits that mediate the corresponding emotional responses.

Again, we are optimistic and energized to further pursue the implications for the structural cognitive changes made possible by the provision of MLE.

SPECIFYING THE RELATIONSHIP
BETWEEN NEUROPLASTICITY AND COGNITIVE MODIFIABILITY

The mirror neurons are the main, but not the only, mechanism for the ability of the brain to be modified by experience. Plasticity works throughout the brain and *throughout our lifetimes*. Our work with individuals with a diverse range of functional levels and adaptive limitations has demonstrated this. It has been described throughout this book. We have described the genetic/chromosomal and the environmental barriers that have been overcome. It is the linkage between the neuralplasticity and the mediated learning experience (MLE) that makes this possible.

But it is the plasticity of our brains that explains the changes that can be produced. New experiences allow the brain to alter existing structures or form new connections to increase functional potential (e.g., increase synaptic density). It is proposed that new experiences are entered into short-term memory and that this sets off a chain of neurochemical and electrical stimulations that effect deeper and more long-term structural changes—what some have termed a neural echo. Ultimately, existing pathways are altered or new ones are formed. Plasticity allows the brain to rebuild connections that are interrupted or underdeveloped by trauma, disease, or genetic conditions.

The implications of these phenomena for cognitive modifiability are immense. Research is suggesting that the human brain can generate new brain cells, even into old age. If the brain is stimulated, at any stage in the life span, it will adapt, regenerate, and become more efficient. It reinforces our initial and ongoing theoretical hypotheses and confirms our methodological developments.

Considering the level of genetic transmission and structures, it has been shown that it is possible to choose from the large pool of genes within the chromosomes that lead to certain types of traits—that is, this pool allows for a choice. It means the genes—even if not modified—can be *chosen*. There is, therefore, the whole scale of potential from changes in the neurogenesis of the human organism—new branch offs and synaptic connections, even migration of cells. This enables us to consider modifiability not only as a very important characteristic of the human being. It permits us to say that the cognitive structure, the personality states, the emotional conditions can all be meaningfully affected by certain kinds of interventions that need to be defined.

An excellent example of these connections is the work of Jeffrey Schwartz (2002), who has extended the concepts of neuroplasticity to addressing problems such as obsessive/compulsive behavior disorders. It opens the potential for modifiability to a broad range of conditions and behaviors.

WHAT IS THE MEANING OF ALL OF THIS?

We are now confronted with a question. What is the nature of the interaction of the organism/environment/brain behavior that is most likely to be responsible for these changes? This has the potential to eventually point to the keys by which such modifiability can be produced.

What are the changes that have to occur in society? Professor Luis Albert Machado, the Minister of Intelligence in the government of Venezuela in the early 1980s, wrote a small book entitled *The Right to Be Intelligent*. He said that if intelligence depends on us—on what we are going to do—then it is the role and obligation of each government to make this available to its people. The implications are that we can no longer act as though we are not responsible for what happens to the student. We cannot say that we are confronted with things that are immutable, therefore we must ask how can we change them. We are, as human beings, given the responsibility and power to correct the limitations placed on our students by genetic inheritance, accident, or environment.

EXAMPLES OF IMPLEMENTING MODIFIABILITY

As a final reminder of the potential for structural modifiability we want to briefly describe some of the meaningful changes we have been able to achieve with those with whom we have worked:

> Mark, a highly functioning architect, suffered a stroke. Initially he could not articulate words and convey his thinking, which was unaffected. After receiving consultations from experts who said that there was little to be done, he worked intensively with FIE over a several-year period. He regained speech, recovered most of his lost or impaired cognitive functions, and has returned to productive—and high level—occupational functioning. Importantly, he has a drive to convey to others the potential that was recovered in himself, in spite of predictions to the contrary.
>
> Alex had the left hemisphere of his cortex removed at the age of 8 in order to eliminate the negative effects of Sturge-Webber syndrome (epileptic-like seizures in the brain that were totally disabling). Because he had not learned to speak prior to the surgery, it was predicted that he would not be able to speak or engage in any higher level communication or thinking activity. As he began to develop, contrary to the neurologist's predictions, there was no explanation for these seemingly impossible developments. Intensive FIE and other forms of MLE, applied from the age of 14, resulted in his developing very complex thinking skills, the ability to learn to read, doing mathematics, and leading to an independent life—including attending a college to learn accounting skills.
>
> Ron, who suffered a traumatic brain injury (TBI) in the frontal lobes, recovered his physical skills relatively rapidly. He then engaged in a 2-year course of FIE that enabled him to start and finish a university curriculum with a double major in psychology and anthropology. He was quoted in a public forum as saying: "You must be careful of Feuerstein, he is dangerous, he will not let you be as you are!"

For us, education is much more than the simple transmission of knowledge or producing skills in the individual. Education should follow the basic contention that human beings can be modified and should be modified, and made able to be more responsive and effective in their environments. Ultimately, this is an answer to the perversities, the criminality, the dysfunctions that are pervading our communities and larger society. How do we best create in the student or individual conditions that enable the expression of a different gene or use of another brain pathway than has been used until now? The implications are immense and demanding.

No one claims that were these implications positively addressed, individuals would be totally equal. But the basic amount of intelligence needed to adapt oneself and change one's responses in order to create and achieve goals, as we have described in this book, are intimately related to finding ways of increasing *intelligent* functioning—again, according to the many parameters we have presented in this volume.

Perhaps the best summary we can make of this potential to intervene and change the nature of human potential is to reiterate the concept of the triple ontogeny of human development that was addressed in Chapter 4. We hold that human beings are not determined only by their biological natures, by their chromosomes, or by their histories of experience in their cultures, their states of deprivation or enhancement. A third ontogeny, mediated learning experience, is needed to fully manifest and materialize the potential for human development. As we pointed out in our earlier discussion, this is as important for normal development as it is in situations of deprivation, dysfunction, and disability.

This point of view makes it possible to accept the strong link between behavior and the brain and to acknowledge the reciprocal effect they have on one another. The knowledge we have today about the ways in which the various neurophysiological components of behavior—the cells, the synapses, blood flow to the brain, electrochemical stimulation—makes the concept of modifiability a neurophysiological phenomenon that underlies and supports the behavioral functioning.

QUESTIONS AND ANSWERS THAT POINT TOWARD THE FUTURE

All this brings the concept of the human as a modifiable entity to a state of understanding through not only logical positing but of experimentally derived (e.g., data driven) conclusions. It is thus elevated to the level of scientifically evidenced phenomena. Among the basic questions that we posed at the outset of this book were: What are the behaviors that will affect and modify not only the nature of the behavior but the structure of the brain (and vice versa)? Which behaviors will best affect the brain to be modified, in cases of deterioration and restoration as well as normalized development? How can we best overcome accidents, adverse conditions, or aging? What are the characteristics of the environmentally determined and observed behaviors that will best affect the neurophysiological conditions of the brain? How can we help students reach their highest potential?

It has been stated that for behavior to affect the brain it must be new and more complex than the usual, familiar, or previous experience. For instance, behavior that is known and is automatized does not affect the neuroanatomy as significantly as does new and unfamiliar behavior. People who just continue to do what they are familiar with—that which they have done for the last 50 or 60 years—will not derive as much benefit from this behavior with regard to keeping their brain undeteriorated by age. When we want to rehabilitate the brain-injured person it is not helpful to repeat that which is known; we need something that is new to become the source of new structures to replace structures that have been damaged. What is needed is a way to formulate the nature of intervention programs, the nature of incoming stimuli, the nature of activities imposed on the brain that will affect not only the behavior but the neural structures responsible for the behavior.

When MLE was described more than 30 years ago, it was identified as the determinant of behavior. When we wanted to explain why children from specific cultural groups, such as the Yemenites, are more modifiable than children from other groups, it was because of the great amount of MLE that is a formidable component in the Yemenite culture. Now, we have another confirmatory and expansive body of knowledge that not only supports the theory of MLE as a major determinant of human behavior, but extends it in directions that we cannot be fully cognizant of at this point in time. Thus, the explosion of science and technology gives us both hope and responsibility!

Annotated Bibliography

This annotated bibliography is included to help the reader who wishes to learn more about the concepts and processes described in this book. The references offer elaborations of the theory and applied programs, with descriptions of practices, illustrative case studies, and various instruments and implementation issues.

Feuerstein, R. (2003). *Theory and applied systems: A reader.* Jerusalem, Israel: International Center for the Enhancement of Learning Press.

> Eight selections from the Feuerstein literature that provide a comprehensive coverage of the main theoretical and applied aspects of Feuerstein's theory. It's appropriate for both novices and experts in the field. Experts will find in-depth discussions of some of the major elements of the theory. Newcomers will benefit from the multiple perspectives offered on both theory and applications of the Feuerstein Instrumental Enrichment (FIE) program, the LPAD, and the shaping of modifying environments (SME).

Feuerstein, R., & Falik, L. H. (in press). *Mediated soliloquy—and beyond: Theory, concept, and a guide to practical applications.* Jerusalem, Israel: International Center for the Enhancement of Learning Press.

> An introduction to the application of structural cognitive modifiability (SCM) and mediated learning experience (MLE) to the stimulation and development of language. Both theory and practices are grounded in support from the new neurosciences. It provides a comprehensive taxonomy of language development to be structured into the provision of mediated self talk (soliloquy) generated by the adult mediator and eventually observed in the children to whom the soliloquy is directed. Practical suggestions are offered about creating language experiences and calibrating responses based on observations of child behavior.

Feuerstein, R., Feuerstein, R. S., Falik, L. H., & Rand, Y. (2002). *The dynamic assessment of cognitive modifiability: The learning propensity assessment device:*

Theory, instruments and techniques. Jerusalem, Israel: International Center for the Enhancement of Learning Press.

An introduction to the theory and applications of dynamic assessment, contrasting it to conventional psychometric methods, and describing the Learning Propensity Assessment Devise (LPAD) as an important alternative approach to assess cognitive functions. A description of the LPAD Standard and LPAD Basic batteries. Practical applications are presented, including group assessment, assessment of special populations, and research applications. Detailed case studies of both individual and groups assessed by dynamic methods are included.

Feuerstein, R., Feuerstein, R. S., Falik, L. H., & Rand, Y. (2006). *Creating and enhancing cognitive modifiability: The Feuerstein instrumental enrichment program* (2nd ed.). Jerusalem, Israel: International Center for the Enhancement of Learning Press.

The second edition has been revised and expanded to include the current developments in theory and practice. The foundational theories and applied concepts (SCM, MLE, deficient cognitive functions, the Cognitive Map) on which the Feuerstein Instrumental Enrichment (FIE) program is based are presented in detail. The instruments of FIE Standard and FIE Basic are described, with applications to classroom and therapeutic populations, research applications, and teacher training included.

Feuerstein, R., Rand, Y., & Feuerstein, R. S. (2006). *You love me! . . . Don't accept me as I am* (3rd ed.). Jerusalem, Israel: International Center for the Enhancement of Learning Press.

This is the third edition of a very popular book that was written to introduce the reader, in an accessible format, to the application of structural cognitive modifiability (SCM) theory and mediated learning experience (MLE) to individuals with special needs—genetic, chromosomal, developmental, and behavioral. The book includes general discussions of the theory, how to apply it in diverse situations, and illustrative case studies. A final chapter has been added to address the issues of inclusion of the special needs individual into normalized environments—an issue of critical importance and vital need.

References

Aebli, H. (1951). *Didactique psychologique: Application a la didactique de la psychologie de Jean Piaget*. Neuchatel, France: Delechaux and Niestle.

Baron-Cohen, S. (1997). *Mindblindness: An essay on autism and the theory of mind*. Cambridge, MA: MIT Press.

Binet, A., & Simon, T. (1905). Methodes nouvelles pour le diagnostic du nivear intellectual des anormaux. *Anee psycholol., 11*, 191–244.

Buccino, G., Lui, F., Canessa, N., Patteri, I., Lagravinese, G., et al. (2004). Neural circuits involved in the recognition of actions performed by non-conspecifics: An fMRI study. *Journal of Cognitive Neuroscience, 16*, 1–14.

Carr, L., Iacoboni, M., Dubeau, M. C., Mazziotta, J. C., & Lenzi, G. L. (2003). Neural mechanisms of empthay in humans: A relay from neural systems for imitation to limbic areas. *Proceedings of the National Academy of Science, USA, 100*, 5497–5502.

Doidge, N. (2007). *The brain that changes itself*. New York: Viking.

Feuerstein, R., & Falik, L. H. (2000). Cognitive modifiability: A needed perspective on learning for the 21st century. *College of Education (San Francisco State University) Review, 12*.

Feuerstein, R., & Falik, L. H. (in press). *Mediated soliloquy: Theory, concept, and a guide to practical applications*. Jerusalem, Israel: ICELP Press.

Feuerstein, R., Feuerstein, R. S., Falik, L. H., & Rand, Y. (2006). *Creating and enhancing cognitive modifiability: The Feuerstein instrumental enrichment program*. Jerusalem, Israel: ICELP Press.

Feuerstein, R., Rynders, J., & Rand, Y. (1988). *Don't accept me as I am*. New York: Plenum.

Fogassi, L, & Ferarri, G. (2007). Mirror neurons and the evolution of embedded language. *Current Directions in Psychological Science, 16*(3), 136–141.

Gallese, V., Keysers, C., & Rizzolatti, G. (2004). A unifying view of the basis of social cognition. *Trends in Cognitive Sciences, 8*, 396–403.

Goleman, D. (2006). *Social intelligence*. New York: Bantam Books.

Harre, R., & Van Langan Rove, L. (1991). *Physical being: A theory for a corporal psychology*. Oxford: Blackwell.

Herrnstein, R., & Murray, C. (1994). *The bell curve: Intelligence and class structure in American life*. New York: The Free Press.

Iacoboni, M., Koski, L. M., Brass, M., Bekkering, H., & Woods, R. P. (2001). Reafferent copies of imitated actions in the right superior temporal cortex. *Procedures of the National Academy of Science, USA, 98*, 13995–13999.

Iacoboni, M., Woods, R. P., Brass, M., Bekkering, M., Mazziotta, J. C., & Rizzolatti, G. (1999). Cortical mechanisms of human imitation. *Science, 286*, 2526–2528.

Kohler, L., Keysers, C., Umilta, M. A., Fogassi, L., Gallese, V., & Rizzolatti, G. (2002). Hearing sounds, understanding actions: Action representation in mirror neurons. *Science, 297*, 846–848.

Kozulin, A., Lebeer, J., Madella-Noja, A., Gonzalez, F., Jeffrey, I., Rosenthal, N., & Koslowsky, M. (2010). Cognitive modifiability of children with developmental disabilities: A multicentre study using Feuerstein's Instrumental Enrichment-Basic program. *Research in Developmental Disabilities, 31*(2), 551—559.

Lesser, G. S., Fifer, G., & Clarke, D. H. (1965). *Mental abilities of children of different social class and cultural groups.* Chicago: University of Chicago Press for the Society for Research in Child Development.

Liberman, A. M., & Mattingly, I. G. (1989). The motor theory of speech perception revised. *Cognition, 21*, 1–36.

Meister, I. G., Boroojerdi, B., Foltys, H., Sparing, R., Huber, W., & Topper, R. (2003). Motor cortex hand area and speech: Implications for the development of language. *Neuropyschologia, 41*, 401–406.

Patterson, F. G. (1978). The gestures of a gorilla: Language acquisition in another pongid. *Brain and Language, 5*(72).

Patterson, F. G. (1981). Ape language. *Science, 211*, 4477.

Rand, Y., Mintzker, Y., Miller, R., Hoffman, M., & Friedlender, S. (1981). The instrumental enrichment program: Immediate and long range effects. In Mittler, (Ed.), *Frontiers of knowledge in mental retardation, 1*, 141–152.

Rizzolatti, G., & Arbib, M. A. (1998). Language within our grasp. *TINS, 21*(5), 188–194.

Rizzolatti, G., & Craighero, L. (2004). The mirror neuron system. *Annual Review of Neurosciences, 27*, 169–192.

Saarela, M. V., Hlushchuk, Y., Williams, A. C., Schurmann, M., Kalso, E., & Hari, R. (2007). The compassionate brain: Humans detect intensity of pain from another's face. *Cerebral Cortex, 17*(1), 230–237.

Schubotz, R. I., & von Cramon, D. Y. (2001). Functional organization of the lateral premotor cortex: fMRI reveals different regions activated by anticipation of object properties, location and speed. *Brain Research Cognitive Brain Research, 11*, 97–112.

Schubotz, R. I., & von Cramon, D. Y. (2002a). A blueprint for target motion: fMRI reveals perceived sequential complexity to modulate premotor cortex. *Neuroimage, 16*, 920–935.

Schubotz, R. I., & von Cramon, D. Y. (2002b). Predicting perceptual events activates corresponding motor schemes in lateral premotor cortex: An fMRI study. *Neuroimage, 15*, 787–796.

Schwartz, J. M., & Begley, S. (2002). *The mind and the brain: Neuroplasticity and the power of mental force.* New York: Regan Books.

Seyal, M., Mull B., Bhullar, N., Ahmad, T., & Gage, B. (1999). Anticipation and execution of a sample reading task enhance corticospinal excitability. *Clinical Neuropsysiology, 110,* 424–429.

Singer, T. (2006). The neuronal basis and ontogeny of empathy and mind reading: Review of literature and implications for further research. *Neuroscience and Biobehavioral Reviews, 6,* 855–863.

Skoyles, J. R. (2008). *Mirror neurons and the motor theory of speech.* Available at www2psy.uq.edu/CogPsych/Noetica/OpenForm Issue 9/

Umilta, M. A., Kohler, E., Gallese, V., Fogassi, L., Fadiga, L., et al. (2002). "I know what you are doing": A neurophysiological study. *Neuron, 32,* 91–101.

Wicker, B., Keysers, C., Plaillyu, J., Royet, J. P., Gallese, V., & Rizzolatti, G. (2002). Both of us disgusted my insula: The common neural basis of seeing and feeling disgust. *Neuron, 40,* 655–664.

Zigler, E., & Butterfield, E. C. (1986). Motivational aspects of changes in IQ test performance of culturally deprived nursery school children. *Child Development, 39,* 1–14.

Index

About the Authors

Louis Falik is emeritus professor of counseling at San Francisco State University (California, USA) and a senior scholar focusing on training, research, and professional development at the Feuerstein Institute (formerly, the International Center for the Enhancement of Modifiability, or ICELP) in Jerusalem, Israel. Since 1985, Professor Falik has trained and collaborated with Professor Reuven Feuerstein in the development and dissemination of Feuerstein's theories on cognitive modifiability and practical implementations. Professor Falik is author and co-author of a number of books and research papers on dynamic assessment (LPAD), the Feuerstein Instrumental Enrichment (FIE) program, and mediated learning experience. He is a clinical and educational psychologist with extensive experience in the training and application of the FIE and the LPAD in child, adolescent, and adult populations, focusing on both learning disabilities and academic performance and enhancement objectives.

Rabbi Refael S. Feuerstein is deputy chairman of the Feuerstein Institute (formerly ICELP) in Jerusalem, Israel. He has furthered the work of Professor Reuven Feuerstein by extending the theoretical and practical applications of programs to materialize structural cognitive modifiability, bringing the practical benefits of this theory to an increasingly diverse range of populations and applications. As deputy chairman, he assists Professor Feuerstein in furthering the conceptual and operational development of the theories of cognitive modifiability and mediated learning experience, and he coordinates professional development activities within Israel and internationally. He is also the primary developer of the Instrumental Enrichment–Basic (FIE–B) and Learning Propensity Device–Basic (LPAD) programs, which are applied to young children and severely low-functioning older learners.

Professor Reuven Feuerstein formulated the theory of structural cognitive modifiability (SCM) and mediated learning experience (MLE) as a response to the need to help the children who survived the holocaust. In the 1970s, Professor L. J. Cronbach said of his work, "[it has] changed the face of modern psychology." Professor Feuerstein founded the Hadassah-WIZO-Canada Research Institute, which became the International Center for the Enhancement of Learning Potential (ICELP) and is now the Feuerstein Institute. He has fostered the development of programs based on his theories and aimed at assessing and intervening in learning and development, and these programs have generated a new field of application—dynamic assessment and the improvement of cognitive functioning. These programs have been disseminated throughout the world and have been translated into more than 17 languages. He continues to develop his concepts, to stimulate scholars and practitioners from all corners of the world, and to see and help children and families.